AMERICA COMES ACROSS

TO ALL MY FRIENDS IN AMERICA—

*In grateful recognition of more
than thirty years of unfailing
kindness and hospitality*

AMERICA COMES ACROSS

BY

IAN HAY

LONDON
HODDER AND STOUGHTON
LIMITED

THE TYPOGRAPHY AND BINDING OF
THIS BOOK CONFORMS TO THE
AUTHORISED ECONOMY STANDARD

First printed August 1942

*Made and Printed in Great Britain for Hodder & Stoughton, Limited, London
by Wyman & Sons Limited, London, Reading and Fakenham*

CONTENTS

PART I

PART II

CONTENTS

TO THE READER

I HAVE just read this little book through at a sitting. This is not to set an example to my readers, if any, but because (for a reason which will become apparent in a moment) this is the first opportunity I have had of doing so ; and, secondly, because I was anxious to see if the volume read as a whole possesses the necessary continuity and cumulative interest.

The last time I wrote a book of personal impressions was twenty-seven years ago. It was called *The First Hundred Thousand*, and was a sort of running chronicle of the adventures of a certain unit (Scottish) of Kitchener's Army, from its hasty and unostentatious birth in August, 1914, to its not undistinguished participation in the Battle of Loos in September, 1915. It was written, one might say, from hand to mouth, in pencil, upon scraps of paper torn from a field dispatch-book, and send home piecemeal by any available means. I never saw the book as a published whole until I came home on leave in the following December, and I remember being agreeably surprised to find how smoothly my disjointed instalments seemed to fit together. And this despite the fact that in the general distraction of those strenuous days I had almost forgotten what the earlier chapters were about.

America Comes Across has been written under very similar conditions of stress and strain—if you are prepared to substitute for the sound of guns the turmoil of urban America. The articles were written from week to week for serial publication in Britain*; each had to be cabled home on a given day and hour from wherever the writer happened to find himself—no light addition to the labours of a speaking tour of some twenty thousand miles.

Now I have returned from the United States just in time to correct the final proofs of those articles in book form. I have not altered or added to them in any way,

* In *The Empire News* : Allied Newspapers.

so they contain none of that all-too-plentiful commodity of these days, wisdom after the event.

Neither have I changed the order in which they were originally issued. In this way I hope the reader will be enabled to follow me in tracing the steps—steps now growing to strides—by which within the past nine months the most powerful single nation on earth advanced along the road from comfortable, almost lethargic, isolation to acute realisation of its own peril and its own moral duty towards the rest of civilisation. (Perhaps it would not be unfair to add that, so far, the average American is more keenly conscious of the latter than the former.)

Of course this tremendous transformation has taken time. You cannot mobilise a hundred and thirty million imaginations overnight. In addition there has been much deliberate and intentional opposition to overcome and many obstacles to surmount. Some of these are described in the pages which follow.

Yet already much has been done, much that we, amid the fog of war, have not always been able to discuss. To-day, as I write, America has sent her sons, with their equipment, to Australia, Hawaii, Great Britain, the Middle East, and Alaska. She is sending supplies to India and China, and supplies and equipment to Russia—all this despite the grievous handicap, shared with ourselves, of shipping shortage, and fantastically long lines of communication. The activities of such industrial centres as Detroit have to be seen to be believed. Her output of munitions of war is now topping our own, and she is gradually overtaking her outstanding problem, transportation. To-morrow, if we are patient and remember our own early struggle towards complete efficiency, we shall see what we shall see. One thing is sure : Uncle Sam is out to end Hitlerism, and when he hits his real stride Hitler will know it.

IAN HAY.

PART I

I

THE LIGHTS OF NEW YORK

I HAVE been in America for just forty-eight hours. I should like to begin by telling you how I got here and how long my journey took, but the Nazi Intelligence Service takes an unhealthy interest in such matters, and I have no desire to oblige them.

I am in New York, which I have known fairly intimately for more than thirty years. Almost the last words which my household addressed to me when I left London were : " How queer it will be to find yourself in a city all lighted up at night," and I agreed.

Now that I have got here it does not strike me as queer at all, for the simple reason that one cannot picture New York as anything but a blaze of illumination. If I were to find myself in a completely blacked-out New York, that would be queer indeed. Well, perhaps I shall before all is over ; you never know in these days.

What does seem strange, almost uncanny, is to realise how completely one has got used to going without the small comforts of life. As soon as you finish the pat of butter on your plate at breakfast here, a waiter hurries up and deposits a fresh one. If you buy a cigar or a small packet of cigarettes, the man behind the counter, according to lavish American custom, hands you a free box of matches. It is most embarrassing to accept such gifts after such long abstinence ; indeed, one feels a little furtive about it all.

9

Meanwhile, what are my first rapid impressions ? Out-standing is the astonishing contrast between the attitude towards ourselves of the New Yorker to-day and of the New Yorker of twenty-five years ago, when I landed on an exactly similar mission to my present one, a prolonged lecture tour upon the subject of British war effort.

In the Great War, so called, our cause found little favour in the eyes of America, as a whole, at first. The affair was regarded very largely as one of those periodical clashes between effete European monarchies in which a sturdy democracy could have neither part nor interest.

The fact that we were as democratic as themselves had not yet been realised by Americans ; they still had a fixed belief that our country was run by a lot of people in spats and monocles. The only Allied country at that time toward which America bore any genuine affection at all was France, who had sent Lafayette over to help to turn the British out of the American colonies more than a century before.

But Russia was the chief bar to American participation. France was France ; England, despite everything the American might think of the English, was England still. But to ask free and democratic America to row in the same boat with the Czar of all the Russias was a little too much.

Lastly, there was a strong impression throughout America in 1916 that Germany was going to win the war. The Allies so far had achieved nothing, and the submarine sinkings were beginning to establish a strangle-hold on our shipping. Neither was our possible defeat entirely regarded as a world disaster of the first magnitude. The German colony in America were good citizens, and the Americans, though they disliked the Kaiser and his jack-booted Junkers, had a proper respect for German business efficiency. Perhaps, too, some Americans felt that it would do John Bull no harm to be deprived of some of his ill-gotten dominions.

In any case, which ever way the Great War went, the New World could stand aloof, unaffected by the troubles and follies of the Old.

But that is all gone now. Even within the brief period of my visit thus far I am conscious of two tremendous changes in American public opinion.

The first is in the American estimate of the British character. For some reason, the average American has been inclined for a generation past to regard the Englishman as too soft, too easy-going, decadent—almost a Wodehouse character, in fact. But that opinion is gone for ever, and a certain reluctant admiration has taken its place. For this we have to thank the civil population of our country, especially the Londoners and the inhabitants of other bombed cities. To a highly-sensitized and imaginative nation such as the Americans are, it is almost inconceivable that any urban population should have endured what our men, women and children have endured for months on end, with such fortitude and philosophy. The verdict is that Britain can take it. That is one of the sincerest compliments that an American can pay. They also realise that Britain can give it. The way in which the Royal Navy have held the seven seas against the Nazi, or in which the R.A.F. have shot him out of the sky, has roused their unstinted admiration.

The other change is this, and it is even more significant. It is now fully realised here, in New York, at any rate, that America can no longer stand aloof from world politics, or claim that the New World is not interested in the fate of the Old. Every thinking American feels in his heart to-day that sooner or later the United States will have to intervene more actively in this war than at present, not necessarily by sending over an expeditionary force, but at least by increasing moral and material support to a maximum degree, and perhaps by sending direct aid, both by sea and air.

But, of course, to believe a thing is not necessarily to admit it. New York and the Eastern States, one gathers, would welcome active participation with Britain. The spectacle of our single-handed struggle against enormous odds excites their admiration and not least their concern. But elsewhere there is in existence a hard core of fierce opposition to any such idea—an alliance, in fact, between pro-German and anti-British sentiment, assiduously fostered by an enormous and highly-organised body of German propagandists within the United States.

To this category must be added the Isolationists, or America First party, who say frankly that they care nothing for what happens to Europe or the British Empire so long as America remains secure and aloof.

The man, of course, whom we are all waiting for in America is the man who has not yet made up his mind; who sympathises warmly with our cause and the cause of human freedom generally, but hates the thought of the dislocation of his own daily routine, quite apart from the suffering and bloodshed that active participation would involve for America as a whole—the man, in fact, who wants to wait and see. But without him America cannot move, and the trouble is that he is waiting too long.

Nobody knows this better than President Roosevelt. But he is determined not to rush his country into war: whatever America does it shall be done unanimously. So he proceeds with infinite caution from point to point. The first news which greeted me upon my arrival in New York, after a longish period during which I had been cut off from news of any kind, was of the President's " shoot on sight " order—in other words, permission to the

American Navy, however neutral in thought it might feel, to open immediate fire upon Nazi submarines or surface raiders in American waters. A big step, especially as the waters in question are obviously to be regarded as an elastic element.

But these, as I say, are only first impressions—New York first impressions. Within a few weeks I hope to visit the Middle West and South—in other words, two remote and entirely different countries.

II

MANHATTAN MIXTURE

MEANWHILE I am occupying this brief lull by re-exploring New York, always a new and fascinating adventure.

New York is quite unlike any other city anywhere, for various reasons. The first is geographical. Although New York ranks as the largest city in the world after London, the only part of it which really counts in the eyes of the New Yorker is Manhattan Island. If you live in any other part of the city, you are not in New York but merely of it.

Manhattan Island is not really an island. It is a peninsula some four or five miles long, and not much more in places than a mile wide. Upon its west side rolls the majestic Hudson River, separating it from the suburb of Jersey City; upon the east is the East River, a much less impressive waterway, with the vast Surrey-side, so to speak, of Brooklyn on its other bank, joined to Manhattan by various bridges and subways.

Brooklyn, for some unexplained reason, is the target

of much Manhattan humour. I once heard a popular
American comedian, possibly Will Rogers, say to an
audience that when he was rich enough he intended
to buy Brooklyn, and close it. No one seemed to
appreciate this aspiration more than the Brooklynites
present.

However, since to be anybody at all in New York,
whether from a commercial or social point of view, you
must have your domicile in Manhattan, that island is
overcrowded to a degree that would make an anthill
look like the Great Sahara. Being incapable of expanding
sideways, Manhattan has, therefore, expanded upward.
Consisting, as it does, of solid rock capable of supporting
any weight, it is covered with pillar-like buildings of forty
or fifty stories, made familiar to us in pictures, each rising
higher than its neighbour until the pyramid is crowned
by the thousand-feet tower of the hundred-story Empire
State Building. From a distance the effect is that of an
almost cloud-capped dream city. At nightfall, with lights
twinkling from a million windows high up in the sky, the
illusion is that of some fairy illuminated mountain.

Thus, by a geographical accident, was the American
skyscraper born. On the whole, New York looks much
more attractive by night than by day. But what a black-
out problem it would present, and what a target for a
night bomber!

Socially speaking, New York, despite its vast size, is a
curiously small place. In London you may encounter a
familiar or famous face almost anywhere—in Hyde Park,
or Trafalgar Square, or Kensington High Street, or in
Piccadilly or the City. But in New York such encounters
are confined practically to Fifth Avenue, which runs up
Manhattan like the middle bar of a gridiron, with the
other Avenues lying parallel, twelve in all. These are
crossed every hundred yards by a numbered street running

east and west. This makes New York the easiest city in the world in which to find your way about.

The Avenues are some miles long, dead straight, and their character changes as you proceed northward. They have their roots in the shipping and banking headquarters at the south end of the island. A few miles farther north they are given over mainly to the shopping and entertainment interest. After that come the residential quarters, ranging from the stately mansions and flats of the so-called East Seventies to the wilds of the Bronx and Yonkers up beyond the neck of the peninsula.

That part of New York which corresponds to the West End of London is confined to a brief stretch of two Avenues—Fifth and Fourth (or Park). If you penetrate a hundred yards or so east or west you will find yourself in surroundings corresponding to those of the Whitechapel Road or Camden Town. But America is a land of sharp contrasts everywhere.

It only remains to mention the last and most famous, or at least the most widely advertised street in all America, Broadway, which runs diagonally across Manhattan Island from south-east to north-west, intersecting every Avenue and cross street at some point or other. Wherever Broadway cuts across the intersection of an important street and Avenue, there you will find an extremely busy square or circle. The most famous and crowded of these is Times Square, which is not a square at all, but a large triangular space formed by Broadway flowing through the intersection of Seventh Avenue and Forty-Second Street. This is the pleasure centre of New York, and of America. Practically every building is a theatre, or a cinema, or night club, or place of refreshment, all jammed together and flowing over.

Then there are the famous Broadway lights, an ever-changing kaleidoscope of neon advertisements reaching high up into the sky. What they advertise no one ever remembers ; people are too fully occupied in enjoying the ingenuity of their design to worry about their purport. To most of us the famous Broadway signs advertise Broadway, and nothing else.

New York, too, is unlike any other city for what may be called racial reasons. It is the most cosmopolitan centre in the world, and is less representative of America than any place on earth. It was once said by an American wit that New York is owned by Germans, bossed by Irish, and run by Jews. Certainly most of the real estate businesses and most of the big hotels seemed to be controlled by German firms ; the Irish contingent, including the police, play a prominent part in politics ; and the Jews e firmly entrenched everywhere where money is to b made, from Wall Street to Broadway, and from Broadway to t! ready-made clothing business, which is one of the staple industries of New York, and gives employment to thousands of poor aliens.

It may be added that most of the skilled workers and mechanics are Italian or Polish. The catering business appears to be divided pretty evenly between the Italians and the Greeks.

The net result of this mingling of races, each contributing to the life and layout of New York the customs and traditions of his native land, is an enormously vital and colourful atmosphere. You see every type of architecture, every style of exterior and interior decoration. The streets themselves are a blaze of colour, with their hundreds of canary coloured taxicabs and ' bright green buses. There is abundance of sound, too, from the perpetual braying of klaxon horns to the strains of music proceeding from the radio set with which every taxicab is fitted. If the chauffeur happens to be a negro, the radio is never turned off at all.

But to the average American New York is just a re-creation centre—the place for a thrill. Sooner or later in his life, however remote his home town may be, he contrives to visit New York, to see the bright lights of that great city. New York knows this, and lays itself out to encourage such traffic. Every omnibus has a legend emblazoned along its side—" Welcome to New York, the Wonder City." Have we ever thought of doing that in London ? No. We take our provincials in our stride, as a matter of course.

But in New York everyone is out on the boost. It begins with the taxi-driver, who conveys you to your hotel. He leans back and converses affably with you through the open window behind him, with an occasional glance to his front as a concession to the fact that we are travelling about forty miles an hour.

But his conversational openings have changed somewhat of late. Not so long ago he merely welcomed you to New York and congratulated you upon your good fortune in being in such a wonderful place. No wonder, for in most cases he himself was an alien, escaped from the squalor and poverty of some oppressed European community to the spacious, roaring freedom of the New World.

But to-day, as soon as your driver has observed that you are British, which he does as you step into the cab, he begins to talk about the war. He is almost invariably pro-British, and says so. He is particularly pleased if he can claim any British connection or blood. His name, by the way, is printed on a card in the cab, and a queer medley these make.

There was Jake Lobel, for instance. He asked if I had ever met his sister in London. She ran a dancing academy which I had doubtless attended, in Battersea. Her name was Madam Lobel, and her establishment was famous. I took his word for it.

Then there was Joe Palotta. He looked like an Italian, but turned out to be a stout enough American citizen.

"Do you know Hull, England?" he asked me. "My wife comes from there. I went to Canada in the last war and joined the Canadians. That was how I came to visit Hull in England. My wife's here in New York right now. I'm glad she ain't in Hull any more. They had a fierce time there from raids. Too bad."

This morning I took a trip in yet a third taxi. The name of the driver this time was Karl Schlitz. We did not converse.

III

PATRIOTISM AND POLITICS

I HAVE already tried to give some impressions of the attitude of New York and the Eastern States of America generally toward ourselves and the war.

I have now realised that East is East and Middle West is very decidedly Middle West. I have recently travelled, spoken, and listened in Ohio and Missouri, both Republican strongholds, and have observed two things. The first is that American admiration for the fortitude and determination of the British people to-day is as great as elsewhere; the second is that in the Middle West you cannot keep war or anything else out of politics.

Two men's names are on every lip in the Middle West to-day. They furnish almost the sole topic of discussion. The first, rather surprisingly, is the name of Lindbergh; the second, needless to say, is that of Franklin Roosevelt.

I will speak of Lindbergh presently: his case is worth special attention. Let us first turn to the President, and his status and character in the eyes of Republican Missouri. Put briefly, it is this. Thousands of Missourians are fully alive to the need of giving Britain all the aid and comfort in their power, and that quickly; but they strongly object to being marched to their goal under the banner of Franklin Roosevelt, whom they dislike as a political opponent and distrust profoundly as a man who, in their view, has tampered with the American Constitution.

In our own country we have no settled constitution to speak of—nothing but a bundle of ancient precedents held together by an extremely elastic band of red tape. But the American Constitution is rigid, precise and sacred. There is no doubt that Franklin Roosevelt stretched it pretty freely in his so-called New Deal, and in the manœuvres by which he engineered his nomination to a third term of office. In the first case he antagonised big business and all believers in orthodox finance, who accused him of giving way to the Labour Unions; and in the second he did a thing which George Washington himself had refrained from doing. His critics to-day add that, having secured his election to a third term in 1940 by playing up the coming war, he is now planning to secure a fourth term in 1944 by suspending the Constitution itself and proclaiming himself dictator for the duration.

How far there is any truth in this last assertion I do not know, but I have certainly heard it made, and more than once. To ourselves it can only be of interest as an indication of how far the President's obvious hope of bringing a united America into the war is likely to be realised. At the moment, and in this great and powerful centre of American opinion, this dream seems far from fulfilment. But political animus is a strange and unaccountable thing. It is also apt to be short-lived. One American warship sunk by enemy action, one bomb dropped on New York or New Orleans, and the ranks may close overnight.

But apart from politics, I have heard much genuine and honest speculation as to America's wisest course to-day. We have friends in the Middle West, and they want to help us to win the war. But they ask: " Do you really think it would be a help, to dislocate the whole industrial life of this country in order to send over an American Expeditionary Force of millions? Wouldn't it be better to keep these young men at home, to speed up the wheels of industrial output for you?"

These are reasonable questions, and they require answering. But they tend to delay immediate action, and this suits the book of the Isolationists—the so-called America First Party—all along the line.

Their attitude is crystal clear. They are out first, last and all the time to keep America out of another European War. The name of England means nothing to them except as that of an ancient foe. American boys must never again be sent across the ocean to pull chestnuts out of the fire for John Bull: and so on.

The nominal leaders of this group are Senators Wheeler and Nye, a pair of elderly die-hards full of homespun virtue but with little knowledge of world affairs. The real spearhead in the attack upon American intervention in the war is that strange, tortured, self-centred visionary, Charles Lindbergh, once the pride and hero of his country, now its most discussed and in many quarters best-hated citizen.

I call him self-centred because he has arrived at his present outlook as a result of deep brooding over his own personal experience of life. Fourteen years ago he was a mechanic engaged in flying commercial aircraft in the Middle West. He was of a dreamy and retiring nature, and only appeared completely at home in the air.

One day he suddenly decided to fly the Atlantic. The feat, it was true, had been accomplished eight years before by two Englishmen, Alcock and Brown, but no one had ever succeeded in a solo flight. So Lindbergh set off, and some thirty-three hours later found himself in Paris. It was a tremendous achievement, though probably no greater than that of Alcock and Brown, who had made their flight in an earlier type of plane, far inferior in design and security. Lindbergh also knew when he set out to fly the Atlantic that the Atlantic could be flown, whereas the two had no such encouraging certainty.

Anyhow, the world went mad about " Lindy." He was fêted in London and Paris, and his own people made a god of him. Wherever he went upon his return to his country he found himself moving in a blaze of adoring publicity.

Then came a tragedy which sounded round the world. He married the daughter of a distinguished American diplomat, and a son was born. The child was kidnapped, held for ransom, and ultimately found murdered. Search was made for the supposed assassin, there was an arrest, a trial and an execution. A fresh wave of publicity broke over Lindbergh, this time of the most morbid and ghoulish type. Wherever he fled his path was beset by hysterical sightseers.

Finally he could endure it no longer. He forsook his native country and sought sanctuary in England. All he wanted, he told us, was to be left in peace. We took him at his word, and unkind people in America say that he never forgave us for it. Anyhow, he soon passed on to Germany. Here he was made much of. Hitler gave him a decoration, and was at pains to send him everywhere to witness the growing strength, good order, and discipline prevalent among the German people. Lindbergh was deeply impressed. No unbridled press, no unrestrained sightseers—just a tidy, efficient, and perfectly regimented world. Above all, a conception and fulfilment of air-development and air-power which thrilled his very soul.

He returned in due course to America convinced of three things. The first was that the British were a soft and decadent race; the second that Germany was the future ruler of Europe and the Old World; the third that democracy was an untidy mess, and that Hitler's New Order was the beginning of a new heaven on earth.

Such was the strange blend and sequence of personal experiences which created the Charles Lindbergh of to-day. With the outbreak of war he immediately joined the ranks of the Isolationists. He has only recently come into prominence, for the sufficient reason that so far no one has regarded him as much more than a simple hero who has allowed himself to become mixed up in politics.

But Lindbergh is much more than that. He has become a leader of men. He can address a great meeting, it is said, and hold it. He can tell the meeting that democracy is dead, and get away with it. He is not afraid to attack the President, and the President has acknowledged his existence to the extent of depriving him of his honorary commission in the United States Army. He is quick to detect vulnerable points. The other day the President, endeavouring to appease certain religious bodies who had their doubts about rendering assistance to " atheist " Russia, stated that in Russia to-day anybody may worship as he wishes. Lindbergh promptly denied this, and started a public controversy which still rages, and is just what Lindbergh wants.

On the other hand, he has recently discovered to his own cost that it is never safe to mingle politics with religion. He recently told a radio audience that the Jews were at the back of an organised campaign to drive the United States into war. That foolish assertion has definitely lost much ground for him.

Still, here he is : he has arrived. He is that most dangerous of creatures, a practical visionary. He speaks only for a group, and a small group at that, but he has made himself the most vivid personality in America to-day. Some denounce him as a national menace who should be put under restraint, others point to him as a future President of the United States. If I get an opportunity I shall go to hear him speak.

IV

ON THE MISSISSIPPI

" A NIGGER and a mule. Yes, sir, there's the South for you, right there."

This rather sweeping generalisation comes from a slick business man, obviously from the North, sitting across the gangway from me in the long open railway coach.

He points out of the window. The train has halted at yet another little wayside station, almost walled in by seven-foot sugar-canes. Outside the station on the dirt road stands a rickety wagon upon which sits a drowsy negro in his undervest and trousers, presiding over the slumbers of an elderly mule.

A hundred yards beyond the sugar-canes runs a low, level ridge silhouetted against the blazing afternoon sky. That is the left bank of the Mississippi River, or rather the rampart or levee which restrains its waters. Our single-track railway follows its course right down to New Orleans, whither we are bound.

Some fifty miles back, while waiting for the train, which was half an hour late, I climbed to the top of the levee and surveyed the great river. Its greatness consists chiefly in its length and breadth; otherwise it is not nearly so impressive as the Nile, or the Indus, or the Hudson. Its brown, mile-wide, slow-moving waters, with their flotsam and jetsam of vegetation and derelict timber, give the impression sometimes of an animated swamp rather than of the Father of Waters. Still, it is one of the great and noble streams of the world, and was once the principal highway of North America.

This train is not one of America's show trains. I hope to describe some of these in a later dispatch. It consists of the usual oversize black locomotive, a mail van, and two coaches, one for whites and one for negroes. In most of the Southern States, where the proportion of black to white is high, the colour bar is strictly observed. Our average speed I hesitate to estimate, but we háve stopped at least ten times in the last hour, at stations with curious French names like Grosse Tête and Point Coupeé, reminders of the eighteenth-century days when Louis XIV held most of that vast and only partially explored domain designated Lousiana, which sprawled behind the English colonies of the Atlantic seaboard.

In due course the young American Republic bought the French out, and in the so-called Louisiana Purchase of 1803 made American occupation of America complete. Several other States have since been carved out of the original Louisiana, but the title still holds good in the existing State itself, which runs for two hundred and fifty miles along the Gulf of Mexico in the South, while the Mississippi winds tortuously down its eastern border to New Orleans.

There are some thirty or forty of us in the coach,

married couples with children, a few commercial travellers, boys and girls on their way home from school, and a group of young officers in the uniform of what corresponds to our O.T.C., obviously prepared to kick up their heels in a week-end's leave at New Orleans.

We are united in one thing, our efforts to keep cool. It is late October, but summer has suddenly decided upon a second innings. When I arrived in New York a few weeks ago, clothed for an American winter, I was saluted by a temperature of ninety in the shade, and it is no cooler here. However, nobody stands on ceremony. We sit sociably in our shirt-sleeves, take a drink of ice-water occasionally from the cooler at the end of the coach, and conversation is general. It always is in this friendly country. It would never occur to an American in a railway train or any other public resort to be stand-offish with his neighbour.

This brings us back to the nigger and the mule. As I expected, the North's aspersions upon the South do not go unanswered. The challenge is taken up at once by the car conductor, a uniformed veteran in gold-rimmed spectacles. He stops playing with a passenger's baby and looks up sharply.

" Where you from, young man ? " he asks.

" Detroit, Michigan—greatest producing centre of——" The old gentleman sniffs.

" Flivvers," he says acidly. " You got any oil up there ? Any cotton, any sugar ? " Before the other can reply he turns to me.

" British, I guess."

I nod. It seems useless to deny it.

" Ever been in Baton Rouge, up the River ? "

" I slept there last night."

" Did you notice the Standard Oil Company's plant along the east bank ? "

I reply that I had noticed it. Indeed, its volume of black smoke had ruined a particularly lovely landscape.

" Well, that's where we're helping you along right now. The biggest oil-refining plant in the world. The tankers come right up there from the Gulf to load up, then down again and right across the ocean to Britain. We got big airydromes there too, with a bunch of your British boys training. Yes, sir." He warms to his subject. " Fine little city, Baton Rouge; the State Capital. Fine men and women. I was raised there. Did you visit the State-house ? "

" It was the first place I was taken to."

" They took you up the tower ? "—anxiously.

" To the very top."

" Fine tower. Yes, sir. Highest building in the South, four hundred and fifty feet. It set us back "—he names an astronomical number of dollars. " Did you visit the Senate—and the corridor outside, where they shot Huey Long ? It chipped the marble some, but I guess that's fixed by now. How's things over in Britain ? "

I told him.

" That's fine. Well, when you write home tell the folks the South's right behind them. Right behind the President too. No, that ain't right; we're way out in front of him. He has to watch his step, I guess; can't go ahead as rapid as he likes on account of some of the States behind kind of slow, with strikes and such." Here the speaker turns a withering eye upon the representative of Detroit, who looks the other way. " Ain't that so, folks ? "

From the demeanour of my fellow-passengers, apparently it is so. I have struck the Solid South, and no mistake. No Republican half-measures here. The man from Detroit would obviously like to put in a plea for Michigan, but decides, rightly, that the moment is untimely. He retires to the end of the car and drinks ice-water.

"You going to New Orleans?" continues the conductor to me, affably. "A fine city—historic. The Paris of America. Now we're moving again," as the train starts off with a sudden jerk, and the nigger and the mule fade from our vision. "I'll be glad to handle your baby for another spell, ma'am."

I am in New Orleans now. It is my first visit for more than twenty years, and the resemblance to Paris is not striking. It never was. Down on the water-front there is a faint suggestion of Marseilles, but that is all. Somehow one is more reminded of Cairo, with the Mississippi substituted for the Nile. There are the same sunny, crowded streets, the same medley of white and dusky faces, the same semi-tropical atmosphere. Oddest reminder of all, you cannot stop for a moment in a New Orleans street to speak to a friend or look into a shop window, without becoming aware of a small uninvited black boy upon his knees at your feet, assiduously "shining" your shoes.

New Orleans has always lived a little apart from the rest of the United States. It was a great and flourishing French settlement when the whole of the eastern seaboard of America was British. This aloofness was maintained even after American settlers swarmed into the city with the Louisiana Purchase. New Orleans even tried to contract out of the Civil War, upon the ground that being French in origin, she had no interest in a war between two purely American communities.

Even to-day, amid a medley of skyscrapers and modernised thoroughfares, the old so-called French Quarter—

the Quartier Carré—survives, with its narrow streets,
stucco-fronted houses, wrought-iron balconies, and green
shutters. But it presents a melancholy spectacle. The
truth is, America is too progressive to be interested in
the maintenance of museum pieces. In America a collection of antique buildings tends to generate into a slum,
and as a slum it must go. To-day most of the French
Quarter has gone, and the rest is going. It cannot con-
tend with a modern thoroughfare like Canal Street, four
miles long and wide enough to accommodate six sets of
tramlines, which cleaves its way clean through the centre
of the city, brushing much of the old French Quarter
from its path.

No, as a centre of eighteenth-century glamour and
bravado, as a resort of buccaneers, as the home of fabu-
lously wealthy slave-owning cotton and sugar planters,
New Orleans has had her day.

But a new day is dawning. The chances of war have
inaugurated a fresh era of material prosperity for New
Orleans. Go up to Baton Rouge, sail along the coasts
of Louisiana and Texas, pay a visit to Oklahoma, and you
will understand. Oil, oil, everywhere. The new commander-in-chief and arbiter of victory is General Gasoline.
Round Oklahoma City, which sprang to life and wealth
only a few years ago, you have only to look out of your
tenth-story hotel bedroom to see more oil derricks than
you can count. There is even one in the city itself, right
up against a Government building. Down the Mississippi
and in from the Gulf this golden stream flows, bringing
to the ancient city and port of New Orleans prestige and
prosperity such as the Buccaneers never dreamed of.

For the last time I take my stand upon the levee and
look out over the Mississippi. Out in midstream is a
long string of scows, carrying crude oil up to the refinery
at Baton Rouge. From the wharves at my feet a squadron

of tankers are setting out across the Atlantic to carry the precious finished article to the Allies. Beside me stand two dock-side labourers. Each displays upon the front of his cap an enormous white button with the legend in black letters—"To Hell with Hitler!"

That is New Orleans to-day, and the Solid South.

V

PERPETUAL MOTION

DURING the past three weeks I have travelled some seven thousand miles by train, a journey equivalent to a trip across the Atlantic and back, and have had a useful opportunity to renew my acquaintance with the American railway system, the most highly organised public service in the world.

It has to be, for thousands of Americans literally live in the train. The reason is plain. The American mind does not take kindly to our deliberate method of conducting business by correspondence, because that involves waiting for an answer. So if a man in New York wants to sell something to a man in Chicago, he jumps into the first train and travels a thousand miles to do it.

The travelling salesman, so called, is an established institution in the United States. He may be the head of a business or an agent working on commission, but whoever he is he thinks nothing of visiting a different city every day for weeks on end. He may put up at a hotel for a few days in some especially important centre, but most of the time he lives, sleeps and moves on wheels.

American business men, and for that matter a large

section of the American public, do most of their travelling by night. In Britain, except for a few express services between London and certain large cities, night travel is practically unknown. One reason is that distances are too short; a night journey is only worth while when it lasts all night, for nobody wants to join a train or leave it in the small hours of the morning. Another is that the accommodation upon our night trains is too expensive at the top of the scale and too uncomfortable at the bottom. A third is that most of our railway companies are in the hotel business themselves.

But American night travel is extremely comfortable and astonishingly cheap. For a price equivalent to that of our third-class ticket and a supplement of a few shillings, the American traveller can pass the night in a real bed, wash and dress in at least reasonable comfort, partake of an excellent breakfast, and step out upon the platform at eight o'clock in the morning as fully equipped for the day's business as if he had emerged from an hotel, which indeed he has.

Moreover, by a really remarkable system of what may be called inter-company exchange, the traveller can proceed by through sleeper from almost any city in America to any other. This may involve him in a certain amount of shunting and bumping during the small hours, but he may sleep secure in the knowledge that when the negro Pullman porter awakens him in the morning he will find himself at his proper destination.

One evening last week I joined a train at Asheville, a remote junction in North Carolina. There were four Pullman sleepers—my own bound for Cincinnati, and three others bound for Louisville in Kentucky, Detroit in Michigan, and Columbus in Ohio. When I arrived in Cincinnati next morning there were still three Pullmans in addition to my own, but these had been picked up at various points during the night, the others having been dropped at their appropriate junctions. Compare that with a night journey by third-class smoker, say, from Bristol to Leeds.

For some reason Americans are constantly condemning the shortcomings of their railways. Perhaps a steady level of standardisation makes for monotony. Certainly every Pullman car ever made is exactly like another. Its interior arrangements have so long been a stock subject for mirth in the movies that there is no need for me to describe them here. The curtains which line the central aisle are a standard shade of sage green, and bear conspicuous numbers, to prevent regrettable accidents. There are two berths, an upper and a lower, in each section, each nearly three feet wide and extremely comfortable. These are allotted without regard to sex or previous acquaintance, but each inmate is so securely tucked away behind his or her curtain that except for certain stereotyped struggles and muffled groans in the darkness above or below you, indicating a fellow creature endeavouring to undress in a horizontal position, your seclusion is complete.

The Pullman porter, or berth attendant, is the most highly standardised product of the whole American railway system. To begin with, he is invariably called George. There are fifty thousand of him, and I never knew one whose technique differed by a hairsbreadth from another's. He is courtly, he is benevolent, and he likes to use rather long words. When he comes to awaken you in the morning, he deliberately tickles your nearest shoulder, with infallible accuracy, through the material of your green curtain. He declines to accept any sleepy announcement that you are now awake. He continues to tickle, respectfully but remorselessly, until you respond by reaching out a hand and pressing the bell-button at the side of your berth. That he will accept as reliable evidence.

When you are dressed and ready to leave the train he offers to " brush you off." As you are going to give him twenty-five cents anyhow, you let him do it, and he gives you six standardised flicks with a whisk broom. After that he produces a duster and " wipes off " your shoes.

If you are extravagant enough to travel in a reserved compartment, of which there are nowadays quite a number in every train, George at once recognises you as a superior being. He addresses you as Colonel, and converses upon seasonable topics. To-day, of course, there is only one. He consigns Hitler to perdition in a few words of several syllables, and expresses complete confidence in the ability of the Allies to attend to the matter. " Yes, sir, ' remarked my attendant to me a few nights ago, " Molotov and Chamberlain sure will fix him." Apparently news does not travel very fast in Pullman circles.

But within recent years the American railways have broken with the past in two marked respects—ventilation and speed.

Nobody who has had to endure it will ever forget the old standardised Pullman car smell—that indescribable blend of disinfectant, chewing-gum and ordinary bedroom stuffiness. Now, however, with conditioned air in perpetual circulation, that horror is banished for ever. As for speed, the past ten years has witnessed a revolution, chiefly owing to the competition of the Airway companies, who will whirl you across the continent in a night. Consequently there has been a brisk tightening up of railway timetables of late. For years the crack train of the United States was the Twentieth Century Limited, which ran daily from New York to Chicago, a distance of a thousand miles, in twenty hours, an average speed of fifty miles an hour. As far as I remember it carried a barber, a typist, and a shower-bath as additional attractions. Such a train, the pride of the New York Central, was not to be rudely invaded by ordinary persons. A red carpet was laid along the station platform when it left, and an extra fare was charged, which was solemnly refunded if the train arrived late.

In other words, the Twentieth Century did for the plutocratic few what the Flying Scotsman had been doing for years, so far as speed was concerned, for the ordinary third-class passenger.

But these jog-trot days are over past. The Twentieth Century, now streamlined, covers its thousand miles in sixteen hours at some sixty-two miles per hour. The other railways have followed suit. You can travel from Chicago to Milwaukee, ninety miles, in about seventy-seven minutes.

Even the long-distance trains to the Pacific coast, which were accustomed to pound along through the deserts of Arizona and New Mexico and over the Rockies at some twenty or twenty-five miles an hour, have been galvanised into strenuous action. There is a train-de-luxe now running twice weekly between Chicago and Los Angeles, and patronised chiefly by luminaries of the film world, which covers the distance in two days and nights. It used to take four.

Meanwhile let it be recorded to the credit of the American railway systems that during my recent trip of twenty-one days of almost continuous travel, I never have missed a connection or failed to find a smiling George keeping faithful guard over my reserved bed.

I hope later to describe some of my human contacts during that pilgrimage, and my own reactions thereto. An American in his vest and trousers brushing his teeth elbow to elbow with you in a Pullman wash-room may look like any other American doing the same thing in another wash-room, but there the resemblance ends. Each State, each township, in this great and vigorous country seems to breed its own type of rugged individualism and personal opinion, especially about the war.

VI

HELPING HITLER

THE war on the American home front, like that on the Russian, seems temporarily to have lost its momentum*— momentum that is, towards active participation in hostilities. Indeed, during the past week the pendulum has showed a tendency to swing the other way.

Of course, in these days of swift and dramatic change the situation may reverse itself before these lines are published, but as I write the Isolationists have two causes for temporary satisfaction.

The first arises from a domestic clash within America itself. Labour trouble in this huge country seems to be endemic all the time. The relations between employer and employee have never been satisfactorily standardised. Trades unionism is not yet an accepted factor in the general scheme of American industrial life, as with us, and no automatic machinery exists for the settlement of disputes. The Labour Unions stand aloof from the employers and the Government, and are controlled by all-powerful and frequently unscrupulous bosses. A few days ago the most powerful of them all, John L. Lewis, personally challenged the authority of the President by calling out fifty-three thousand coal miners whose work was vitally essential to the production of steel. The output of important war material is in consequence seriously jeopardised. Nobody knows this better than Lewis, and the strike which he has called is, quite frankly, an attempt to coerce the President into immediate acceptance of Lewis's terms, instead of awaiting the decision of the arbitration board now sitting.

* November, 1941.

Other strikes are in progress in other industrial centres. Some are on a large and, from a military point of view, a regrettable scale. For instance, a great aeroplane factory in New Jersey has been immobilised for some weeks, and military aid has now been requisitioned to enable those who wish to work to do so.

Other and smaller strikes serve to indicate the tendency of war conditions to cause what may be called wage dissatisfaction. Visit almost any American city to-day and you will encounter little processions of shabby men and women parading up and down outside a shop or restaurant, holding aloft improvised placards which announce that such-and-such a firm is UNFAIR, in capital letters, to Organised Labour; or that they are the employees of a certain business concern and are on strike for Better Conditions—again in capital letters.

These demonstrations are permitted by law, as long as the demonstrators keep moving and do not indulge in direct action. Sometimes they go on for weeks. They are not important in themselves. Many of them are frank attempts to blackmail the firms concerned. The men and women with the placards are outsiders hired for the day. But some are probably justified, and they undoubtedly give an impression of disunion at a time when all should be united. They are part of the price that democracy has to pay for its free institutions.

The big strikes, however, are a direct menace to war effort. The American people have no sympathy with them whatever, and probably few of Lewis's followers have any real desire to be unpatriotic. They just do what they are told. Consequently an argument is raging as to what ought to be done to Lewis. The majority of the people say that he ought to be in gaol. Others go further, and point out that if only the President would declare war upon Germany, then Lewis could be shot as a traitor.

The Isolationists refrain from comment, because Lewis is playing the game for them, and they know it. The President's political opponents, however, seize this opportunity to assert, not for the first time, that in canvassing for a third term he involved himself so tightly in the toils of the Labour bosses that he dare not strike back.

The President himself has adopted his own and, as usual, rather unexpected line. He has made a personal appeal to Lewis as a patriotic American to call off the strike, and allow the dispute, whatever its merits, to be adjusted by constitutional means.

Lewis, after a day or two of studied indifference and aloofness, has now majestically agreed to discuss matters with representatives of the National Defence Mediation Board. Even as I write comes the news that the strike has been postponed to November 15th. It is a tactical gain for Lewis. Still, November 15th is a fortnight away, and by that time much may have happened. America may be at war, and Lewis eligible for a firing-squad. For the moment, though, his nuisance value persists, and the Isolationists rejoice.

Such matters as these, of course, are entirely an American concern, but here is one which is not. Within the past few weeks there has been revived and circulated, not by the responsible American from or upon responsible platforms, but by underground suggestion and in street-corner comment, the old, old cry that Britain is once more reverting to her traditional policy of sacrificing her Allies and holding back her own troops. This device, as I say, is not new. When I was in this country twenty-five years ago during the last war, the air was thick with sarcastic assurances that England would fight to the last Frenchman—a suggestion, by the way, which some of the French representatives in America did little to discourage. Not even our million dead, of whom more than eighty per cent. came from England, could entirely dispel that wicked calumny.

And now it is being exploited again. The Fifth Columnists here, with the full force of the German propaganda machine to back them, are proclaiming to America that England will fight to the last Russian.

The point to observe is that responsibility for this particular suggestion does not lie in America, but at home in England.

A few days ago the American press began to publish reports to the effect that the British Labour Party were in full revolt against this Government's lack of aid to Russia, and that the Cabinet had been tersely informed that they must either invade Occupied France as a diversion or make way for more resolute leaders. There was also an impressive description of a monster meeting in Trafalgar Square.

To those of us who know our London and our Britain these alarming rumours amounted to practically nothing at all. From the names cabled over it was obvious that this so-called revolt was limited to the usual handful of House of Commons extremists, reinforced upon this occasion by a section of the general public who genuinely sympathised with the sufferings of the gallant Russian people, and to whom nothing seemed simpler or more obvious than to dispatch an expeditionary force to France forthwith.

In reply to numerous friendly but anxious inquirers here it could only be pointed out, firstly that the leaders of the so-called revolt in no sense represented British public opinion, and that a seaborne invasion of a strongly defended hostile coast is to-day the most difficult operation in warfare. Finally, that we were already sending to Russia assistance in men and equipment on a scale which was actually jeopardising our own safety, and that the Russian Government fully recognised the fact.

The comments of the American press, too, were restrained and sensible. It was pointed out with truth by one widely syndicated military writer that democracies are always slow at getting into a war, but once in, they clamour for quick results and progressive success all the time. That is not how wars work out. Victory, especially if you start half prepared, is a long-term business. The writer also stressed the impracticability and uselessness of an attempted diversion in Western Europe.

But American newspaper readers study headlines rather than the solid sense printed beneath them. Besides, things look different over a distance of three thousand miles. The average American cannot distinguish between our Labour Party, solid to the core for victory, and the antics of a disgruntled handful. In New York, too, where public demonstrations on a large scale are immediately broken up by the police, a mass meeting of Communists in Trafalgar Square, which we are accustomed to regard as one of the ordinary free shows of a London Sunday afternoon, sounds like the beginning of the end.

Thus do mountains grow out of molehills. There is no doubt that this agitation has for the moment done our cause infinite harm. There is a tendency to regard a country which will not help its allies as not worthy of help itself. Two or three of my American friends in the north-west have told me that they cannot conscientiously remain members of the local British War Relief Committee.

With whom does the responsibility lie ? Not with the British nation as a whole ; certainly not with the British Labour Party. Not with the American press, who have treated this matter with conspicuous sanity and fairness. It lies jointly at the door of a handful of unthinking sentimentalists at home.

So we see how easy it is to become the instruments of

your country's enemy, whether you be an American labour boss or a British political crank.

But even as I write, Hitler, the arch-blunderer of all, has gone far to heal the break. He has at last succeeded in sinking an American vessel of war, the *Reuben James*, and already new headlines have displaced the old.

VII

AN EVENING WITH LINDBERGH

ONE day last week I was lunching in a New York club of which, in accordance with hospitable American custom, I have been made an honorary member for as long as I stay here. I said to my neighbour at table :

" I see Lindbergh is to speak at Madison Square Garden to-night."

" Not only Lindbergh," he replied, " but Wheeler, Nye, Cudahy, Flinn—the whole Isolationist circus. It's about their last kick, I guess."

" Are you going to hear them ? " I asked. My companion's face of horror gave me my answer. However, I continued resolutely :

" I should rather like to go. Have I any chance of getting in ? "

" You might get within two blocks of the building. After that not a hope without a ticket. Eight hundred police have been called out to protect these traitors."

A member on the other side of the table addressed me unexpectedly :

" Here you are," he said, and handed me a numbered and reserved ticket for the meeting. A dozen accusing voices assailed him.

" Dan, what are you doing with that ticket, anyway ? "

" It was mailed to my home by the America First Committee. I suppose they wanted their audience to include just a few people from a respectable neighbourhood."

" And they had to pick you ? Well, well, well ! "

My benefactor was still under heavy fire when I left. But I had got my ticket.

" Doors open at six. Meeting at eight. Come Early," said the ticket. This seemed good advice, so I arrived before seven, having dined on a glass of milk and two doughnuts at a lunch counter in Seventh Avenue. As foretold at the club, the Garden itself, in Eighth Avenue, was completely encased in a box-barrage of policemen. However, my ticket acted like a charm, and within five minutes I was in my seat.

Madison Square Garden is about the size of our own Olympia, and holds twenty thousand people. They were all there. Many of them had come in delegations representing this or that Chapter of the America First League. They displayed banners proclaiming the fact. Occasionally they left their seats and marched up and down the aisles. As I entered, I encountered a procession proclaiming that Staten Island was " 83 per cent. for peace." I could have told them of another island where we are 100 per cent. for peace, but not at that price.

The German tongue was much in evidence throughout the Garden. I also observed a phalanx of Japanese, sitting together and industriously waving small American flags, a surprising spectacle even in this medley of contradictions. There was a sprinkling of people who had obviously come, like myself, out of sheer curiosity. But the majority of the audience was composed of women, all shrill and excited to the point of hysteria. There were young women in fancy costumes, distributing flags and buttons. There were elderly women by the hundred, representing the so-called Mobilised Mothers of America, come to protect their sons from being sent to fight England's battles for her. One of these sat next me— a grim old lady clasping in her arms an American flag wrapped round a pole about five feet long. She regarded me with hostile suspicion from the start, which was not allayed when my seat was claimed by someone with a ticket identical with my own. Indeed, there had been trouble with duplicate tickets all evening. Either the Isolationists had been making sure of a full house, or else the opposition had decided to contrive a little diversion. For myself, I stuck to my seat, and my would-be supplanter disappeared in the general confusion.

A platform stood at one end of the Garden, with a speaker's rostrum fitted with a microphone. The forest of instruments usually erected by the various broadcasting companies was conspicuously absent. The great America First Rally had been boycotted by every Radio Corporation in America.

Between the platform and the audience stood a solid and unbroken line of policemen, over whose protective heads the speakers subsequently preached the gospel of America First.

The noise was deafening. Below the platform a brass band played without ceasing, its efforts being intensified by loudspeakers everywhere. White-coated vendors of hot dogs, peanuts, and ice-cream cried their wares. Screaming processions raged up and down the aisles. I glanced wearily at my watch.

At last, after some extremely ragged community singing, ranging from " Columbia, the Gem of the Ocean " to " The Daring Young Man on the Flying Trapeze," the platform party arrived, half an hour late—a bad piece of stage-management, for most of the audience had been waiting for more than two hours.

The proceedings opened, somewhat unexpectedly, with a so-called Invocation by a clergyman, who concluded his offering by bidding us rise and repeat The Lord's Prayer. He pointed out, a little unkindly, I thought, that this would be a good opportunity for those who did not know The Lord's Prayer to learn it.

After that we came to earth with a bump, and the next hour and a half were devoted to good honest Billingsgate, directed in about equal proportions at the Allies, the President of the United States, and all Americans who considered it America's duty to help in ending Hitlerism. " America must not get into a European war," was the main theme. The possibility that a European war might get into America seemed to occur to no one.

The theme was played, of course, with variations. The chairman, after roundly abusing the radio corporations for ignoring the meeting, said that eight million American boys must not be torn from their homes and sacrificed to restore the Dutch East Indies to Holland, and enable England to go on " plundering " India. Senator Nye, who followed him, put the number of prospective victims at ten millions, to the loud approval of my mobilised mother with the flagpole. The next speaker, a former American ambassador to Poland and Eire, told us that the war could be ended to-morrow if Mr. Hoover were permitted to call a peace conference of all nations, with himself in the chair. Hitler, he added, dared not resist such a move. The German generals would *compel* him to agree—a statement remarkable even in that welter of unreality. It was greeted with the usual shrieks of applause, but I was conscious that these were getting a trifle mechanical. The senatorial tub-thumpers were growing monotonous : the audience wanted Lindbergh.

But apparently Lindbergh's time was not yet. First we had to rise to our feet and make a series of promises, raising our right hands and speaking in chorus after the chairman. We promised to write to our Congress representative and our Senator. I rather think we promised to telephone to the President of the United States as well. Under the compelling eye of my next-door neighbour, I rose and recited with the rest, oblivious of the fact that I possessed neither a congressman nor a senator of my own.

Then a collection was taken up. An enthusiastic lady in the platform party led off by offering 500 dollars if someone else would do likewise. Most of us, however, confined ourselves to humbler offerings. I found myself confronted by an attractive young person attired, for no particular reason that I could see, in white shorts, white top boots, and a species of military shako, rattling a collection box.

" I guess you wouldn't care to contribute," she said doubtfully, surveying my too British exterior.

" Why not ? " I replied, and gave her ten cents. " I'm having a swell time."

At long last, about ten o'clock, after a series of nonentities of either sex from the platform party had been introduced to the audience and taken a bow, we came to Lindbergh—tall, boyish, diffident—who had been sitting between two Senators for more than two hours, wearing the distracted smile of the man who has to make the speech of the evening, but is having the wicket spoiled for him by others.

He rose, and the meeting let itself go at last. They howled, they whistled, they waved their flags. Adoring young women almost swooned. For full five minutes pandemonium reigned, augmented by the efforts of the band, which had sprung to new and raucous life.

At last they sat down. Lindbergh produced a manuscript, came to the microphone, and began to read, in a pleasant, well-modulated voice.

In this procedure he differed, to his own disadvantage, from the practised demagogues who had preceded him, who preferred to keep their eyes upon the audience rather than upon their text. He read rapidly, making no attempt to force his points or work up applause. He suggested a self-conscious young college student reading a prize essay, rather than a heaven-born leader issuing a trumpet call to the faithful. To be frank, he was a near flop. If he had not been the speaker of the evening, I think some of the audience would have called it a day and slipped out.

But the substance of his words was in striking contrast to their delivery. Two things were made plain. The first was that the speaker entertained a profound belief in—and admiration for—Adolf Hitler; the second, that he cherished an equally high opinion of Charles A. Lindbergh. Such phrases as, " I decided that this war could end only in a victory for Hitler, or in a ruined and demoralised Europe "; or, " I consider that American intervention would be disastrous to Europe, because Europe must work out its own future "; or, sublimest egoism of all, " In 1939 I advised the Allied Powers to allow Hitler to invade Russia without declaring war," give a fair picture of Charles A. Lindbergh's naïve belief in his own worldly wisdom and importance. Above all, it was the speech of a convinced Nazi. And—there was not a word of sympathy for—or gratitude to—Britain, which had afforded Lindbergh shelter and tranquillity during the most tragic years of his life.

The audience listened, but did not react. They were not really interested in a treatise upon the international situation. They had come either to cheer or to boo. And at last, towards the end of his speech, their hero gave them their chance. He announced that America, mighty America, was for ever safe from danger from without. " But not from within ! " he suddenly boomed through the microphone. There was an answering yell as the crowd rose to its feet. " Impeach the President ! " some women screamed. At last our twenty thousand Isolationists had got what they really wanted—a chance to boo that resolute man, Franklin Delano Roosevelt.

The speech ended immediately after, amid much noise from the auditorium and handshaking upon the platform. Then it was announced that Senator Burton K. Wheeler would speak.

All I knew of this statesman was that he came from a remote State in the North-west, was the high priest of the American First Movement, and had made a speech five hours long in the Senate in support of his principles the previous day. I glanced at my watch ; it said half-past ten.

I rose, evading the eye of the lady on my right, and silently stole away, accompanied, I fear, by several hundred Isolationists.

VIII

THE LAND OF CONTRASTS

PUBLIC opinion in America always seems to be contained in watertight compartments. In other words, the country is so vast, and its nerve-centres so far apart, that every State, almost every city, is a law unto itself, and seems neither to know nor to care what the man on the other side of the State border is thinking or saying.

In our own small island we can, if need be, arrive at

a unanimous decision overnight. But the United States is not a country : it is a continent.

I have had this fact very strongly impressed upon me this week. A few days ago I was in Boston, the capital of New England, whose people are perhaps nearest to ourselves, not only in kin but in habit of mind, of all the American nation. Their ancestors were the Pilgrim Fathers, who left their native land not for adventure or profit, like the Elizabethan aristocrats who founded Virginia, but in search of freedom of conscience a century later.

They landed at Plymouth Rock in Massachusetts, and to-day they inhabit the States of Massachusetts, Maine, New Hampshire, Connecticut, and Vermont, a country of brown grass, stunted undergrowth, and stark, naked rocks. What a perfect camouflage these must have furnished to the Indian braves whom they found there, and against whom they fought for their very existence for nearly two centuries. Thriving cities have now sprung up throughout the length and breadth of this great domain —cities with familiar, homely names like Portsmouth, Exeter, Bedford, Dover and Worcester—but the primeval background remains, as rockbound and unyielding as the New Englanders themselves.

Of course the New Englanders, though nearest to us in character, have not always been near us in sympathy. It was in New England that the American War of Independence was born, with the famous Boston tea-party. But there is no doubting the sympathy and appreciation of New England at this moment.

I was in Boston for Armistice Day, as the guest of the Governor of Massachusetts. The occasion was a Preparedness Parade, and the Governor was there to take the salute. For two hours and a half I stood beside him, in company with a small group of State officials and military officers, upon the steps of the golden-domed State Capitol facing the historic Boston Common, watching a procession three miles long pass by.

The Americans have a passion for pageantry, and they like to be in the pageant themselves. The parade therefore was fully representative, to say the least of it. It was preceded by two little touches, each characteristically American in its thoughtfulness and good sense. The Governor descended from the steps and publicly shook hands with a group of elderly women waiting by. These were Gold Star Mothers, each of whom had lost a son in the Great War. Then, just before the parade began, a loud-speaker car, marked "Police Educational," passed along the route, warning the spectators to keep to the sidewalk, advising them of better view-points, and encouraging them to pass the children up into the front row.

Then came the procession, headed by smart upstanding contingents of regular soldiers, sailors and marines. They were followed by older troops wearing new and business-like green uniforms. These were the State Guard, corresponding almost exactly to our Home Guard. They have taken the place of the National Guard, who correspond to our Territorial Army, and like them have now been absorbed into the Regular Army.

Next came a long stream of ex-soldiers. America is prolific in ex-servicemen's societies, and all of these were represented. There were the Veterans of the Spanish War of 1898, there were the so-called Veterans of Foreign Wars, and there was the American Legion, an enormous and politically powerful body with a chapter or a post in almost every American parish. There were also the Sons of all these Veterans, some of them very juvenile indeed, in various organisations and fancy uniforms of their own. There was a fleet of ambulances and various contingents of Red Cross Nurses. Every section of the Parade carried the Stars and Stripes at its head, and each was preceded by a band. I counted seventy bands before I gave up, and we must have saluted the flag upon an average once a minute. Altogether a most stimulating and colourful scene. It was a refreshing contrast to the Lindbergh rally I recently described. It was real, it was sincere, it was American.

But the parade was not by any means over. Now came an orderly multitude representing the business, social and religious bodies of the State. There were Catholic Church Schools—Massachusetts, with its large Irish element, is the most strongly Catholic State in America—there were patriotic Negro societies; there was even a company of Chinese, headed by a brass band of Chinese girls.

And I must not forget the drum-majorettes. Almost every band in the second half of the parade was headed by one of these, sometimes by half a dozen of them— attractive young persons dressed in white shorts and tunics, white cowboy boots, and an enormous shako. They strutted, they pranced, they pirouetted. Occasionally one of them turned a somersault. Most of them did a special turn for the benefit of the Governor's party.

"Do you like it?" asked the State Treasurer, on my left. "Does it strike your formal British mind as being on the frivolous side?" Then he went on before I could reply: "But believe me, there's more to it than that. These people are here to show that they mean business where Hitler is concerned, and this is the way they show it, because it's the way that suits them. They get on the band wagon. But they are right behind Britain and the President all the time."

The procession halted for three minutes, to let cross-traffic through, and we were able to sit down and relax.

I pondered my neighbour's remarks, and my thoughts, perhaps by force of contrast, went back to the last parade at which I had assisted, as a casual spectator this time, a few weeks ago.

It was in a great city more than a thousand miles farther west, where I was waiting for a train connexion. Darkness had fallen, but the streets blazed with light, for all shop fronts were illuminated. Flags were everywhere. All traffic had been suspended, and the endless lines of parked cars which obstruct every American street had been cleared away by the police. The sidewalks were packed close with spectators, men, women and children, all in holiday mood. The procession was not due to pass for another hour, so the roadway itself was occupied by the more youthful section of the community, improvising demonstrations of its own. Young couples danced to the accompaniment of an impromptu saxophone band. Apparently every American boy can play that distressing instrument. Others wove their way in and out of the throng in what is known as a snake dance— a single file procession, each member of which keeps his hand upon the shoulder of the man or girl in front of him. Small negro boys performed antics of their own. A solid phalanx of white revellers marched by, goose-stepping, and with right hands held aloft, chanting " Heil Hitler ! " This humorous effort was greeted with roars of laughter. I wonder how it would have been received in Boston.

By this time I had discovered from a friendly bystander that we were attending the sixty-seventh Parade of the Veiled Crusader. There was a familiar and slightly sinister ring about this. I associated it in my memory with stories of the Ku-Klux-Klan and other secret societies of the past, with their night-ridings and summary administration of rough justice. I decided not to press for details.

At last the procession arrived, preceded by the

inevitable band and headed by the Crusader himself. He was seated upon the summit of a lofty gilded car, which I shrewdly suspected of having once belonged to a travelling circus, drawn by four horses. He wore long flowing robes and a Viking's helmet, with gilded wings. His face was entirely covered by a veil.

The car blazed with light furnished by the Municipality itself, down an electric trolley-pole attached to the back and kept in running contact with the street-car wire overhead.

More bands and more cars followed, and my suspicions about the circus were amply confirmed. Every car was a circus car, and its occupants were dressed as clowns, lions, tigers, and performing monkeys, who waved greetings to the spectators. There was even a property elephant. At the very tail of the procession, somewhat unexpectedly, came a group of the grotesque figures so common in Riviera carnivals—tottering giants ten feet high, with nodding mask-like heads.

Towards train time I edged my way out of the press and picked up a taxi in a side-street. Our road to the station was frequently blocked by departing sightseers. We pulled up for the tenth time, and the taxi driver cursed the Veiled Crusader with all the resources of an admirable vocabulary.

" Who exactly is the Veiled Crusader ? " I asked, when he paused for breath. " He and his friends seem to have a big pull in this city. Some powerful secret society, I suppose ? "

" Secret society hell ! " replied the taxi-driver simply. " This is just a Chamber of Commerce racket, gotten up to bring folks into the city and spend money. It lasts three days. To-morrow night there's to be a ball, and a Beauty Queen. And I bet the Beauty Queen will be the jane whose old man kicked in with the biggest subscrip-

tion. Well, I guess we got to make your train, Mister."
He blew a blast upon his horn, let in his clutch, and scattered the followers of the Crusader like chaff.

Well, there we are. Whole-hearted enthusiasm for world freedom on the one hand, and complete detachment from all world problems on the other. The Continent of Contrasts.

IX

CROSS CURRENTS

PUBLIC interest here this week has suddenly been switched from the war to the American home front. This is not altogether surprising.

I was travelling by train a few days ago through a district in Pennsylvania which is one of the chief coal and iron centres of the United States. In appearance it is not unlike that part of Lanarkshire which embraces Coatbridge and Airdrie. But those collieries were idle. In other words, the coal strike which had threatened some for weeks, was an accomplished fact. It was limited at the moment to some fifty-three thousand miners in Pennsylvania and West Virginia. Pickets were out, and already there had been clashes and shooting. Most serious of all, this particular quality of coal was essential to the production of steel, and munition plants were threatened with an immediate shortage of material. Bad news for us and good news for Hitler.

A curious wave of unease is sweeping over the United States at the present moment. All the soft-coal miners, three million strong, are threatening to come out in sympathy with their fellows. The railway workers have demanded higher wages to meet the increased cost of living, and a railway strike upon a wide scale has been provisionally fixed for December 7th.

Expert opinion takes the view that this latter strike will not eventuate. The threat has been put out as a feeler, and the matter will probably be compromised.*

The coal strike is in a different category. In the first place, its effect upon the output of war material is immediate and serious, and in the second, the strike itself was but the culmination of a long and bitter campaign.

The issue, according to John L. Lewis, the head of the American Federation of Labour, is a perfectly simple one. The miners are out for a closed shop; in other words, no non-union labour must be employed in the coal industry. Compel the five per cent. of the fifty-three thousand who are non-union men to enter Lewis's tabernacle, and there will be no more trouble.

To this the Government replies that to hold the nation to ransom at a time of acute emergency in order to get the better of an industrial argument, is an unpatriotic and traitorous act, and cannot be permitted.

This view is strongly supported by the public as a whole. Lewis is the most unpopular man in America at this moment. His appearance upon a news-reel is greeted with boos and hisses—a favourite method of expressing likes and dislikes in this demonstrative land. But he is in a strong position, and he knows it. "If you want coal," he points out, "the miners are the only people who can get it for you. You may send the army to take over the pits, as you threaten to do, but soldiers can't dig coal with their bayonets."

To us, fighting for our existence, such a hang-up at such a time seems unthinkable. But the stark realities of war are not easily discerned over a distance of three thousand

* As it turned out, something else happened on December 7th—PEARL HARBOUR.

miles. Moreover, America is at least a generation behind Britain in the handling of industrial problems. Trades unionism and the closed shop are to-day part of our accepted scheme of industrial relations. The machinery of conciliation exists for us in perpetuity, whether in war or peace.

But in America employer and employed still fight with the gloves off. Each side is strongly organised and equally ruthless. Employers are frequently tyrannical, but the tyranny is not all on one side. Only last week two labour leaders were sent, at long last, to penal servitude for blackmail. For years, it was proved, they had been extorting money, running into millions of dollars, from the heads of certain moving picture companies for " protection "— in other words, for graciously refraining from calling a periodical strike of the company's employees.

As usual in an emergency, all eyes have turned upon the President and Government. It is believed that both are privately in favour of the closed shop, though only in due course and after reasoned discussion, and not at the point of a pistol. Public opinion demands an immediate and final settlement, and Lewis knows that if he presses his advantage too hard, Congress may be goaded into some immediate anti-strike legislation so drastic as to put him out of business altogether. He knows, too, that the miners themselves have no particular stomach for a strike. When all is said and done, they have no desire to help Hitler ; so as I write he has suddenly agreed to call off the strike for the time being and submit the matter to arbitration.

But the strike is merely a symptom of something much wider and deeper. America, for the moment, is in the doldrums ; in fact, she is passing through a phase of public sentiment strongly resembling that which seems to prevail in Britain itself—namely, the reaction following a let-up or lull in the course of a great war. That lull, of course, is not apparent to the American sailors and airmen, any more than it is to our own, but its effects upon the army and the industrial workers are plain to see.

A year and more ago, when Europe was rocking, and even Britain seemed fated to lose her ancient liberties, Franklin Roosevelt issued a trumpet call to the American people. Civilisation, he said, was in danger. America must rouse herself, realise her responsibilities, and come to the help of civilisation, especially of the British nation, who were by this time fighting alone. If Britain fell, he indicated, it would be America's turn next.

We know how that call was answered. Compulsory military service was approved and brought into immediate operation throughout the United States. Vast new munition plants sprang into being, while existing industrial machinery was converted to warlike usage. The people were told that they must work harder and for longer hours, and they did. The Lease-Lend Bill was passed. British War Relief Societies worked overtime.

But recently we have struck a patch of smooth water— deceptively smooth water. The Russian campaign seems to have arrived at a winter stalemate, with Leningrad and Moscow uncaptured. The Battle of the Atlantic has taken a favourable turn ; air raids on London have for the moment ceased. All this has been more than sufficient to bring about a slackening of effort in America, human nature being what it is. The danger seems less real, more remote. There is a tendency to sit back and relax, above all to begin to think about oneself instead of one's job. Soldiers and civilians alike are inclined for the moment to regard the Defence campaign not so much as a matter of urgent necessity as a mere measure of precaution—and there is a world of psychological difference between the two.

Even Congress is suffering from a passing wave of

disgruntlement. A few days ago the Bill to permit American ships to ply direct between America and Britain, which has hitherto been strongly backed by Congress as a whole, only passed in the House of Representatives by eighteen votes. Many of the President's steadiest supporters voted against him. This is not attributed to any slackening in approval of the Bill. It was intended as a rebuke to the President for his lack of firmness in handling the labour situation.

Needless to say, the Isolationists and Fifth Columnists are seizing their opportunity to fish in troubled waters. Last week I found myself in a considerable city in the Middle West, well within what may be called the Chicago sphere of influence. The local newspaper published two cartoons on successive mornings. The first depicted a football match, in which Stalin is being badly pummelled by Hitler. John Bull sits on the sidelines, shouting encouragement. "Stick it out as long as you can, Joe," he bawls, "and then I'll send in Sam here to take your place." In the other cartoon we see John Bull again. This time he is digging a grave. The headstone lies ready beside it. It is marked "Second American Expeditionary Force." Not far off stands another and older grave. It is marked "First American Expeditionary Force." The old story—England will fight to the last American!

But when all is said and done, this is merely history repeating itself. Twenty-five years ago, in 1918, America had joined France and Britain in the Great War. But the first flush of enthusiasm had died away. Effort was becoming stereotyped and mechanical There were no strikes, but in the munitions factories men were "lying down on their jobs." Output was being seriously curtailed. Something had to be done.

So a British officer with war experience was sent to

one large industrial centre. He spoke in fourteen work-shops in two days. He described to the men the situation on the Western Front, and the effect upon the enemy of " a present from Uncle Sam " in the form of a new and intensified shell barrage. Touch an American's pride in his country and his job, and he will perform prodigies. These workmen suddenly came to life again and set about their task with renewed zest. At one centre they marched out of the shops in a body, saluted the American flag which was flying outside, and marched back to their work singing.

As I write comes some welcome news from Libya. That should go far to end the doldrums.

X

HOMES ACROSS THE SEA

WE are in a square room surrounded by thick plate-glass windows. One of these looks into a second room, where men wearing earphones are adjusting mysterious-looking pieces of electric apparatus. Through the others you can see a large hall in which a number of people are assembling. Some of them are standing just outside the windows, looking in at us. In other words, we are in one of the studios of the National Broadcasting Company of America, in the city of Providence, Rhode Island. It is Sunday morning.

Eight British boys and girls, ranging in age from six to fifteen, are sitting about the studio. They are here to broadcast to their parents at home. For the moment they are inclined to be a little shy of one another and of their surroundings. They are accompanied by their foster-parents.

The official in charge of the proceedings is going round

with a list, checking up names. Yes, everybody is here, though some have come from a considerable distance. Rosemary and Christopher, for instance. Rosemary has travelled from a large girls' school in Connecticut, and her young brother from a boys' school in New Hampshire. They have not met since they first arrived in this country as evacuees from London, more than a year ago.

Now the foster-parents depart to the outer hall, followed by a few regretful eyes. A little moral support at this point would be welcome to some. To Sonia, possibly. She is only six years old, and the baby of the party. But she sits down placidly enough with the others, while "Uncle George," as we will call him, explains what is going to happen, and suggests various topics of conversation, because experience has taught him that youthful broadcasters, after the first rapturous greeting, are apt to run painfully short of material. He hands round sheets of paper.

"Write down things to say," he advises. "Tell the folks how you're liking it at school, and what games you play, and how much you've grown, and how you find our hot-dogs and ice-cream sodas over here. Things like that. Don't ask about bombs, because they won't tell you. Everybody got a pencil?"

No, it appears that Sonia has not. I offer her mine. She accepts it without comment, and after a brief interval, apparently for manners, hands it back. Obviously she prefers to rely upon the inspiration of the moment. Her action does not go unobserved.

"I believes," whispers one Charlotte to her neighbour, one Hamish, "she's deaf and dumb. She hasn't said a word to anyone." Charlotte is twelve and hails from Hendon. She is a vivacious child and a little inclined to be managing. Hamish, aged ten, is from Glasgow. He considers Charlotte's suggestion, then replies gravely:

" I do not think that they would select a pairson to broadcast that was deaf and dumb." That puts Charlotte in her place.

But time is getting on, for it is nearly twelve-thirty, and the broadcast is due to begin on the stroke of one. To us now enters Uncle Ben, the announcer, who will act as master of ceremonies while Uncle George, in conjunction with the technicians in the next room, attends to the business end.

Uncle Ben sits down with the children and engages in easy talk with them. He is sizing up their radio personalities. It is half the battle in these broadcasts to start off with your most dependable performer.

He is obviously a master of his job. His tactful investigation being concluded, he arranges the children in a row along one side of a baize-covered table, where they sit solemnly facing us, like a miniature court-martial or a very junior board of directors. Before each of them lies a pair of earphones. It is significant that Hamish has been placed on the right of the line, the post of honour. Charlotte and her younger sister Jane are next to him. Sonia is on the extreme left.

The two uncles now proceed to fit the earphones to the appropriate heads ; one or two of these latter are very small, and considerable adjustment is needed. The boys are comparatively easy to fit, but Jane gets into difficulties at once, for her ears are encumbered with a mane of black hair. An uncle renders first aid. Charlotte, needless to say, equips herself completely before anyone can do anything about it.

Now it is ten minutes to one. The uncles themselves don earphones, and Uncle George, taking up a microphone, waves his hand to a watchful person on the other side of the control-room window. Next moment he is greeting the B.B.C. in London—someone called Roy, who happens to be a friend of mine—as easily and nonchalantly as if the B.B.C. were in Providence instead of Portland Place. Roy greets him back, and they exchange small talk while the necessary contacts are being obtained and the pitch adjusted. The children, listening in through their ear-phones, are deeply impressed, and well they may be, for the whole business is sheer white magic, even to hardened broadcasters like myself.

It is exactly one o'clock, and the N.B.C. works to the split second. No easy-going British moments of grace here. Uncle George, after making a formal announcement into the microphone, hands it to Uncle Ben, who takes it over to Hamish. He gives that young gentleman's name and age, and announces that Hamish will now talk to his friends in Scotland; then swiftly places the instrument in the little boy's hand.

By this time I am in the control room, for in the studio, though I can hear what the children say, I cannot hear what they hear. Across the studio I can see the foster parents peering anxiously in through the other windows. They, too, can hear the conversation, though they cannot take part in it. Hamish is proving himself a wise choice for first wicket. He is completely self-possessed, if a trifle cautious in his utterances. As a Scotsman he understands values, especially the value of conciseness in a two-minute conversation. He is talking to his father now.

" Aye," he is saying, " it's great out here. I was in a camp for three weeks. That was great, too. I've lairned to swim. I've swam a mile," he adds, with the calm satisfaction of a man making a statement which no one can check. Uncle Ben leans over his shoulder and gently takes the microphone. " I'll need to stop now. Good-bye, father."

" Good-bye," says father. " And we're glad to have heard your wee voice, Hamish."

By this time Charlotte has seized the microphone, and, head to head with Jane, is dispatching a hurricane greeting to her mother in Hendon. Needless to say, she is fully primed, and makes full use of her two minutes. She reports phenomenal progress in her own learning, stature, and favour with the American people. Jane gets an occasional word in. Once more Uncle Ben applies the closure.

" Good-bye, darlings. Those are the nicest words I've heard for sixteen months," says the voice from Hendon, with a suspicion of a quiver in it.

All this time a press photographer is crouching before the table, taking flashlight close-ups of our young broad-casters. But not one of them even notices him. They are by now completely absorbed by the business in hand—

And so it goes on. Christopher and Rosemary, who appear to be great cronies, have drawn up a joint pro-gramme. Christopher talks to his father, who sounds like a retired cavalry colonel, about the fish that he has caught. Rosemary asks her mother for home items of domestic interest, and inquires eagerly after Iris, Peter, Aunt Lollie and Mr. Scroggs, who, it appears, is a dog.

Incidentally, it is interesting to note how far the children have picked up the American mode of speech. The girls show little traces of it in their accent, though they employ plenty of American colloquialisms. A certain Frances, upon being informed that she now has a baby sister, replies, " How cute ! " and adds, to the obvious incredulity of her relatives, that she has "made" the Politeness Prize at school.

But the boys speak the American tongue almost fluently. Probably they do this to avoid comment or criticism from their schoolmates, who are apt to regard English undefiled as a form of affectation. For instance, Timothy, aged fourteen, informs his mother in Plymouth that he now weighs a hundred and eight pounds and is sixty-two and half inches tall.

" I'll work it out later, dear," says his mother resignedly. " But you're much older and bigger. I can feel that," she adds with a half-sigh.

The extreme case is furnished by Albert, of Grimsby, aged twelve. He has obviously modelled himself upon his own conception of an American gangster. He talks out of the corner of his mouth. He says, " Howya doin' ? " and " Oh, yeah ! " and " So what ? " " O.K." is too unsophisticated for him ; he says " Oke " ! In short, it is to be feared that Albert is showing off.

All are enjoying themselves now, but one is not so certain about the people at the other end. The very fact that we cannot see them gives poignancy to the effort some of them are making, of the front they are putting up. Fathers are strangely boisterous, mothers oddly vivacious. Intimate topics and confidences are kept at arm's length. Everything at home is going on all right, and we are winning the war. Everyone sends love. Jimmy has had his tonsils out, but is going on splendidly. Yes, we have lots to eat, so don't worry. Harry is in the army now, in Kenya, or he would send his love as well. Dad will be in uniform, too, soon. Won't he look funny ? Only when the final " God bless you ! " comes, is a slight weakening of morale audible.

Most moving of all is the obvious eagerness of these parents to convey, within the few moments at their disposal, some adequate measure of gratitude to the people who are taking care of their children. Not one of them omits to do this, and happily the foster-parents, listening in behind the plate-glass windows, can hear their actual words and voices.

Well, time is nearly up, and only Sonia has got to speak. Uncle Ben places the microphone in her small hands, and with a reassuring pat on the back, puts her on the air in due form. Her colleagues and her preceptors all look a little apprehensive. Nobody wants to end up a succsesful seance with a flop.

" Maybe Ben will tell her something to say," says the man at the controls hopefully.

But Ben's services are not required. Sonia emerges from her shell. She greets her mother affectionately, and informs her that she is very well and is wearing a new green taffeta frock, white socks, and new shoes. She adds that after the war she would welcome some arrangement under which she could bring Uncle Joe and Auntie Ruth (her foster-parents apparently) home with her, for keeps. One feels that she should have had the politeness medal instead of Frances.

Then she asks for her father, and says : " Hallo, Daddy, I'm very well and I've lost two teeth."

" Don't lose any more," replies daddy, " or you'll lose your boy friends, too. You've got a boy friend, I suppose ?"

" Yes. But—but—every time I goes near him he runs away ! " Sonia's voice rises with all the fury of a woman scorned, but is drowned by a roar of laughter from the entire studio.

" Well, well," remarks the man at the controls, " the little stooge turned out to be the star of the whole act ! "

PART II

XI

UNCLE SAM AT WAR

SEVERAL times of late impatient Americans have said in my hearing : " We are taking this war too darned easily. We got to get mad."

Well, Americans are feeling mad enough to-day. Neutrality has gone with the wind. America is at war, and at one.

Everything has happened with astonishing suddenness. Only last Sunday I found myself assisting at an after-lunch discussion by a group of New York businessmen as to what would be the outcome of the prolonged conferences then being held between the Cabinet at Washington and the Japanese envoys, with a view to establishing more friendly relations between the United States and Japan. Opinions differed considerably. One man said that he was strongly sympathetic, in theory, toward Japan and indeed all Eastern Nations. " ' Asia for the Asiatics ' is Japan's motto," he said, " and why not ? What right have we in Manila, or Hongkong ? If we want lasting peace in the East we ought to hand the Philippines back to the Philipinos, and the British should hand India back to the Indians."

" Well, let the Japanese make a start by handing China back to the Chinese," said someone, and that line of argument came to a close.

Next came an upholder of conciliation and appeasement. " Japan wants just two things," he said, " room to expand, and a little civility from the white races. Face-saving means a lot in the East. Go to the Japanese, treat them as equals, offer them a loan of a billion dollars and the promise of facilities for territorial expansion after the war, and you'll get them away from Hitler and the Axis right now."

" Where exactly are you going to let them expand territorially ? " asked someone.

" Oh, a big island in the East Indies : Celebes, or somewhere. Nobody particularly wants a place like that."

This policy was held to be too vague altogether, and the company reverted to what they had originally set out to discuss, namely, whether America could best help the Allied cause by coming right into the war, or by maintaining her present position as an arsenal and source of supply. Some said that the sooner Uncle Sam's hat was really in the ring the sooner the war would be over. Others expressed an opinion that an America at war would be bound to divert to herself munitions at present being sent to Britain and Russia, thus weakening the common battle front at its most vital points. To this it was replied that America's resources are unlimited, and that with proper organisation of industry she could supply not only herself but every Ally present and future to the limit.

So the discussion went on. It was all interesting, and all extremely academic. On only two points was there complete unanimity—firstly that Japan had not the slightest intention of risking war with the United States ; secondly, that the American Navy was invincible.

Then somebody switched on the radio for the six o'clock news, and we came down to earth. Even as the two smooth-voiced Japanese envoys held Washington statesmen in parley, Japanese bombers had winged their way across an apparently unguarded Pacific, and Pearl Harbour—the great American Naval Base in Hawaii—had been laid by all accounts in ruins. Japan had not only risked war with America, but had struck the first blow, and if rumour spoke correctly, had won the first round.

The first reaction in New York on that historic Sunday evening was one of astonished incredulity. That Japan, in the midst of peace negotiations, should have been treacherous enough to stab America in the back, and impudent enough to make war upon America at all, seemed beyond belief. The second reaction was that of sardonic satisfaction. " Well, they've asked for it, and Uncle Sam will see that they get it," was the prevailing sentiment. Perhaps this was best summed up by an elevator-boy in my hotel, who remarked to me, as we shot skyward at bedtime :

"Well, dem Japs has the gall to bomb the United States ! I guess they'll get well taken care of now ! "

Monday morning brought sober realisation. The bad news from Pearl Harbour was confirmed, with reservations that were more alarming than a plain statement of fact. In any case the bombing raids were no mere impudent gesture ; they were part of a vast plan of grand strategy. America was at war not only with Japan, but with the entire Axis. *The New York Times*, in a wise, dispassionate and most timely leading article, was at pains to remind its readers of this fact. It said :

"We must not forget that Hitler, and not Tokyo, is the greatest threat to our security. The real battle of our times will not be fought in the Far East. It will be fought in the English Channel."

Then came noon, and the President's address to Congress. Half the world must have listened in to it. In the room where I found myself we rose to our feet as he began. He was brief—he spoke only for six and a half minutes. He was earnest, and he was profoundly impressive. He confirmed, without comment or detail, the news of a very serious reverse at Pearl Harbour, and of widespread damage elsewhere. He emphasised, though, that Japan's initial advantage had been gained entirely by treachery, and could not be repeated. America would win the final victory, " So help us God."

His words blew away the mists and made the prospect clear. From that moment America knew where she stood and what she had to do. By Monday evening every trace of faction and divided opinion had vanished through out the country. Months of argument, intrigue, subterfuge were ended at last, and a sigh of relief ran round the land. As a popular columnist put it, in the vernacular of Broadway :

"Bunk, baloney, apple-sauce, expediency and double talk were blown right out of our National atmosphere by what happened on Sunday."

Meanwhile the Isolationists, headed by Wheeler and Lindbergh, had had a busy day recanting. "America is at war," they announced. "There is nothing now that patriotic Americans can do but fight." The fact that they themselves were directly responsible for serious discouragement of national unity and delay in national preparedness they had conveniently forgotten. I doubt if America will forget so easily.

Since then events have followed what may be called a normal course. One might almost be back in London in September, 1939. There are crowds of young men outside the recruiting stations. A.R.P. preparations are being hurried on. No one seems quite certain how great the danger of an air-raid may be. New York seems remote enough in all conscience from every air-base, but the events in the Pacific and a rumour that Japanese aircraft have appeared over San Francisco have brought it home to New York that nothing is impossible in the air now-a-days.

On Tuesday afternoon of this week we had our first air-raid warning. No one knows whether it was a mere false alarm or a sly experiment by the authorities. At any rate, the results were very much what might have been expected, and what we ourselves have experienced. The majority of the people did not hear the warning at all, which is not altogether surprising considering the medley of piercing noises amid which the New Yorker

south of the line lie the great islands of the East Indies, and to the south of these, most vital and momentous to ourselves, the northern coast of the Commonwealth of Australia.

The first and most important link in the chain is the group of islands known as Hawaii, about as far from San Francisco as Eastern Canada is from Britain. Its capital, Honolulu, on the island of Oahu, can be compared in size and importance with Portsmouth or Plymouth. Here is situated Pearl Harbour, the principal American naval base in the Pacific. Honolulu is the first port of call for the trans-Pacific air services, and is a favourite resort of American tourists, as we know from our own dismal experience of hula-hula films and ukelele moanings.

Next comes Midway Island, so-called because it lies almost exactly on the opposite side of the earth from Greenwich, on the one hundred and eightieth meridian, where, whenever you cross it, you must be prepared to accept, say, two consecutive Mondays or else jump from Monday to Wednesday, according to the direction in which you are travelling. Then Wake Island, not much more than a coral reef, a mile square, and then Guam. Midway, Wake, and Guam are each about thirteen hundred miles apart. Another seventeen hundred miles, and we reach the Philippines, America's most important commitment outside America. The islands were captured from Spain in the Spanish-American War of 1890, but since 1935 have enjoyed what we would call Dominion Status under a President, Emanuel Quezon.

A rough arithmetical calculation, therefore, reveals the fact that the distance from California to the Philippines is more than double that of Britain to the United States ; which gives us some idea of the vast width of the Pacific and the perilous length of the American chain of defences.

While we are considering distances, it is important to

note that Tokyo is nearly two thousand miles from the Philippines, and fifteen hundred from Guam, a formidable hop for bombing aeroplanes. But with the Japanese occupation of French Indo-China upon the Asiatic mainland only five hundred miles to the west, the air menace is rendered serious and imminent. Guam, too, is a weak spot, for it is a considerable island, about the size of the Isle of Man, and has never been properly fortified. President Roosevelt urged as long ago as 1935 that this vitally important work should be put in hand at once ; but the combined forces of economy and appeasement were too much for him. The defensive chain already described is but part of a still longer chain, of which Britain is responsible for the western extension, which runs from the Philippines to the Federated Malay States, with the naval base of Singapore at its southern tip.

Such is the vast ocean battlefield upon which this new and unpredictable campaign must be fought out. Already our two countries have suffered grievous initial losses. The *Prince of Wales* and the *Repulse* are gone, with a tragic toll of lives, and ships in the American Pacific Fleet. The struggle, therefore, will be long and stern, and must for some time be conducted upon purely defensive lines.

But sober and thoughtful Americans are not cast down. On the contrary, they are encouraged by one shrewd and salutary reflection. " Our most dangerous weakness as a nation," said an American friend to me the other day, " is our overwhelming belief in our ability to lick creation. This sudden and early reverse has been a real bracer. It has knocked all our false confidence sky high. Now we can go to work in real earnest and quit accepting promise for performance. That set-back at Pearl Harbour has been worth almost a battle squadron to us. Now that we have learned our lesson and taken our medicine we shall be a different people."

Meanwhile the American home front is in a fever of activity, and history is repeating itself—the history, that is, of any democratic country which finds itself suddenly plunged into war, as we ourselves have good cause to know. Everyone is anxious to help, and no one quite knows how to set about it. There is particular eagerness for information regarding Air Raid Precautions, and British visitors with personal experience of bomb-dodging are greatly in request. There has been the usual sudden run upon blacking-out material and electric torches. Municipal authorities are rehearsing air-raid warnings, upon various lines and with mixed results. Numerous voluntary bodies have sprung into being, for first-aid and the like. Presently, with the American genius for organisation, all these activities will be co-ordinated. For the moment civilian effort must proceed along the hard but sure road of trial and error.

Meanwhile the Government has lost no time in mobilising the resources of the nation. All male citizens between the ages of eighteen and sixty-four must register for national service. Of these, all from nineteen to forty-five are liable to serve in the armed forces. Production has been speeded up. All munition plants will now work a twenty-four-hour day for seven days a week. At present only about fifteen per cent. of the industrial energy of the country is being devoted to the output of engines of war. This will ultimately be stepped up, it is intended, to over sixty per cent. Never has such a power house been set in motion in the world's history, and the American people mean to see to it that the machinery is operated to the limit. Japan's unprovoked aggression has ensured that. It was a psychological blunder of the first magnitude, for it has sent President Roosevelt into action with a hundred and thirty million people at his back, united to a man.

XIII

AMERICA'S HOME FRONT

THE first flush of wrath and indignation over the Japanese onslaught on Pearl Harbour has now subsided, and the American people are adjusting themselves to the practical business of warfare—as yet almost entirely defensive warfare.

The Government has made public the losses incurred upon that fateful Sunday last December, and it is frankly admitted that the army (which in this country includes the air force) and navy were caught, to employ the popular and unusual expression, with their pants down. The general and admiral responsible have been temporarily relieved of duty, and a strong Board of five experienced officials has been appointed to institute what Americans call a " probe," and allocate responsibility.

So far, Japan fills most of the American horizon—so much so that only yesterday the Secretary of the Navy, Mr. Knox, in an address to the cadets at the Naval Academy at Annapolis, referred to the Pearl Harbour incident as " the first great engagement of the war " ! Recent Allied successes in Russia and Libya, which would have been blazoned across the front pages of the American press a few weeks ago, have been relegated to more modest positions, under the heading of " British and Russian claims," and their places taken by the exploits of the American Marines at Midway and Guam, or of individual American airmen. All this is natural enough, and national perspective will soon adjust itself.

The principal and growing preoccupation of the American people to-day is the possibility of air raids. These are more than possible; they are highly probable sooner or later, if only upon a nuisance or, to employ another American term, a token scale. Suicide is much in the air. There are perpetual rumours of Japanese "suicide bombers," who deliberately crash themselves against their chosen objectives in order to make certain of a direct hit, and of "suicide submarines," manned by two men who deliberately sacrifice their lives as well as their vessel by discharging their solitary torpedo at a range of a few yards. On the same principle, it is considered that small "suicide squadrons" of Japanese or German bombers may be expected to load up with much petrol and a few bombs and so contrive to cross the Atlantic and inflict a token raid upon New York, Boston or Philadelphia, and then crash or surrender. At the present juncture, however, anything in the shape of the intensive and continuous bombing to which London and other British cities have been subjected is considered to be out of the question.

Still, there is no doubt that a few token raids would have a most disruptive effect upon the life of the American community and the output of munitions. Responsible individuals, such as mayors, schoolmasters, and proprietors of large department stores and factories, are rightly concerned about it.

And in comparing American problems of home defence with our own, we have to remember this. The hysterically criticised Treaty of Munich at least gave us a year in which to prepare. By the end of that time we had air raid shelters, gas masks, and a completely organised system of A.R.P. We even had hospital accommodation prepared for three hundred thousand prospective air raid casualties. America, on the other hand, has been brought into the war overnight, and is starting from scratch.

The outstanding difficulty, as always in this land of individual ambition, is that of effectual co-operation.

Every little community here, every little group there, wants to run its own show.

America, owing to its vast size, is a country of conflicting authorities. Beginning at the top of the scale, we behold the Federal Government at Washington. Washington might issue a standard code of civilian defence rules and set up a central authority to adminster them; but this Washington will probably refrain from doing, for the simple reason that there are forty-eight States in the Union, and every State is a law, a very jealous law, unto itself, with its own Governor, Senate, and House of Representatives. Moreover, a set of rules which might suit the maritime State of Maine admirably might prove a complete superfluity in remote Arizona.

Then, within each State are a number of cities, and here the State legislature is up against municipal resistance. The mayor of an American city is a very different individual from the picturesque and acquiescent figurehead so familiar to ourselves. He is a politician, with his party at his back. He controls all city finance, all appointments, and the police. Yet even he is not omnipotent. He has to reckon with the American passion for founding societies for the promotion of civic liberty, progress, reform and uplift generally. In every city in America to-day innumerable such organisations have sprung up, all animated by the highest motives, but sadly inclined to get in one another's way, and, in particular, in the way of constituted authority. A distinguished British visitor to this country, speaking in New York a few nights ago, said: " I have already met here within a few days a greater number of committees, mostly self appointed, than in all of England in two and a half years of war-time."

Thrice blessed, then, is a community which can produce a central authority resolute enough not only to deal with the work in hand, but to over-ride a multitude of conflicting counsellors. New York possesses such an authority to day in its mayor. His name is Fiorello La Guardia.

Fiorello is the Italian for "Little Flower," and this sobriquet is applied to "His Honour" (which is an American mayor's official title of courtesy) by friend and foe alike, whether in affection or derison. La Guardia is a typical product of this land of opportunity. His father was a bandmaster in the Italian army. He himself is American born. He served with distinction in the American Air Force in the last war. To-day he is Mayor of New York, which means that he wields in his own person about as much power and patronage as the whole of the London County Council.

He is small, tubby, voluble, and a dynamo of energy. He turns up everywhere, and is particularly fond of attending fires. Like the young man in the song, he flies through the air with the greatest of ease. Indeed, he has to, for his appointments are so numerous and widespread that only an aeroplane can enable him to cope with them. He is a born fighter, and knows every move in the political game. Indeed, some of the methods by which he recently secured his re-election to office are open to criticism by political purists, if there are any in America. But as an administrator he is honest, kind hearted, and capable—in short, about the best mayor that New York ever had. President Roosevelt has recognised the fact by appointing him, even although he is a Republican, a member of his "War Cabinet."

The mayor has a weakness for appearing in topical films and haranguing the audience as to its civic duties. His appearance, and his emphatic gestures and grimaces, are greeted with laughter, but his words get home. He is especially concerned at the moment with air raid precautions, and, like most enthusiasts, is inclined at times to strain his statutory authority. He has announced, for instance, that any New Yorker neglecting to take cover in an air raid, when advised to do so by a policeman, will be liable to a fine of five hundred dollars or a year's imprisonment.

As I write, he has just been summoned to Washington, where it is rumoured that he is to be hauled over the coals for taking it upon himself to stage false air-raid warnings in New York last week, instead of leaving that duty to the army, and in particular for organising a special street-clearing exhibition by the police for the benefit of the news-reel companies. But he will come out on top, for he knows his job, and, above all, he understands the psychology of the American people.

Such is the home defence situation in America to-day—a multitude of volunteers, but no particular machine to harness them to. Proper organisation, of course, is merely a matter of time. A large number of superfluous and conflicting amateur bodies will have to be eliminated first. Indeed, they will probably eliminate themselves—patriotic enthusiasm is frequently a plant of fragile growth—and their places will be taken by compact and efficient bodies of paid workers. That is the only way in a long-term war, as we ourselves have discovered.

Meanwhile the most unhappy people in the United States to-day are its Japanese inhabitants, or any one who looks like a Japanese inhabitant. I sat opposite to a spectacled Oriental gentleman in the subway to-day. He was wearing a huge button on the lapel of his coat, which said plaintively : " I am Chinese, please." He informed me that these buttons are issued officially by the authorities to *bona fide* Chinese residents, at a charge of twenty-five cents per button, the profits going to Chinese war relief. Thus the claims of self-preservation and charity are happily combined.

XIV

THE COMMON CAUSE AND THE ANCIENT GRUDGE

MR. CHURCHILL'S visit to Washington has set the seal upon an alliance, an alliance which has never happened before, and which at various times in our joint history would have been unthinkable.

In saying that it has never happened before I am really stressing the fact that in the last war, the so-called Great War, the United States never entered into a formal alliance with anybody ; neither did the United States declare war upon Austria or Bulgaria or Turkey. Germany was the sole enemy, and it was against German troops upon the Western Front and German submarines in the Atlantic that American forces were exclusively directed.

There was, of course, close and friendly co-operation whenever occasion arose, and eventually all the Allied armies were united under the supreme command of Marshal Foch. At sea also an American Battle Squadron under Admiral Rodman served as a unit of the British Grand Fleet. It was never in action, for the German High Seas Fleet never came out of port again after the lesson of Jutland in 1916 ; but the American Destroyer Squadrons, under Admiral Sims, did brilliant work in conjunction with the British destroyers based on Queenstown.

Upon the Western Front American participation was confined chiefly to General Pershing's A.E.F. on the right or southern flank of the Allied line ; but not entirely. Two American divisions, the 27th and 29th, from New York and Tennessee respectively, served under a British General, Rawlinson, in our Fourth Army, and participated in the brilliant operation by which the Canal du Nord was crossed and the Hindenburg Line broken, in September, 1918.

Still, in the main and on the whole, French, British and Americans took their own line and fought their own battles.

But we cannot afford to do that this time. The war has come full circle round the globe, and there are a score of fronts to be covered where formerly there were two or three. None of the Allied Powers has an army, navy or air force large enough to attend to all those fronts; there must be a careful and appropriate division of labour, and a steady and continuous pressure upon all points at once, so that the enemy will never be permitted to release forces from one theatre in order to avert danger in another. In the same way an allied country must not hesitate, if need be, to send help to a hard-pressed neighbour, even to the detriment of some scheme or campaign of its own. In other words, the war can only be won upon a world-wide, closely-co-ordinated, and faithfully executed plan of grand strategy. There must be no attempt to score points individually or outshine this ally or that. It must be all for one and one for all.

That, presumably, is why Mr. Churchill has visited the United States. He had two tasks to perform. The first was to convince the American people, or such of them as had still to be convinced, that the enemy is Hitlerism in general and not Japan in particular—in other words, that though you may defeat Japan, Germany will remain; while if you destroy Hitlerism, Japan can be automatically liquidated.

But with Mr. Churchill's sudden and dramatic descent upon the shores of America, American press and public were at first less interested, inevitably, in his message than in the man himself. The tremendous, almost legendary, figure whom for nearly two years they had been watching across three thousand miles of ocean, battling single-handed in what seemed at times a hopeless struggle against the powers of darkness and barbarism, was actually in their midst. America, that land of hero-worship and the human touch, clamoured for a " close-up." When the Prime Minister appeared at the President's daily press conference in the White House, the reporters and feature-writers present were at pains first to describe not so much what he had to say as how he looked. They remarked that he had " doffed the seafaring garb " which he had worn upon his arrival the previous day—the uniform of an Elder Brother of Trinity House—and was wearing striped trousers, a black coat, and a blue-and-white polka dot bow tie. " He had his glasses stuffed into a breast pocket, with a service bar upon his left lapel." They described his cigar, of course, and the " pink and healthy tinge " of his complexion. They also noted that he was shorter than they expected. So anxious were they to miss no detail of his appearance that those at the back of the room called to him to rise and show himself. Mr. Churchill, who must have been enjoying himself hugely by this time, and who possesses an unerring instinct for the right gesture, at once complied and, for good measure, stood upon his chair.

But, apart from all this natural enthusiasm and " human interest material," the most notable and significant feature of the press reports of this particular conference was the reference, which ran through nearly every description, to the circumstance that the Prime Minister of England and the President of the United States found themselves sitting in friendly conclave in that very White House which the British had burned in the War of 1812. Indeed, the conference itself was held almost upon the exact anniversary of that inflammatory episode.

The significance of the reminder lies in the fact that

whereas not one Englishman in a hundred to-day has ever heard of the War of 1812, and not one in a thousand knows that British troops once set fire to the White House, American memories upon the subject are very much longer. Englishmen, of course, know that England lost the American War of Independence in 1776, and that there-after the American colonies became the United States of America and had to be written off as a total loss to the British Empire; but concerning the War of 1812, which was fought during our life-and-death struggle with Napoleon, we are very vague indeed, partly because the pages of our history of that time are filled by the story of Wellington's triumphant Peninsular campaigns, and partly because the War of 1812, after more than two years of indecisive conflict, was broken off by mutual consent and with entire lack of advantage on either side.

But these two wars are the highlights of American history. To the average Britisher they denote not much more than a single regrettable incident in Britain's long and variegated colonial experience, and as such are most conveniently forgotten. But to every American they mark the birth of the American nation and the foundation of the American ideal. No wonder the scene in the White House last week roused the American reporters to vivid recollection.

Incidentally, few Americans are aware that the burnings of Washington and the White House by British redcoats was an act of not entirely unjustifiable retaliation for the burning of York, now Toronto, by the Americans in their attempt to conquer and annex Canada some months pre-viously. But that is how patriotic history is written, and few historians, whatever their country, are guiltless in this respect.

Those old unhappy days are only recalled here because

they bring us to Mr. Churchill's second and infinitely more difficult task, the mitigation of what has been called The Ancient Grudge—the traditional suspicion and distrust of most things British in American minds to-day, especially in the Middle West and West. In the Eastern States, which geographically lie nearer to London than to San Francisco and spiritually are in comparatively close touch with the British way of life and point of view, the feeling is much less strong. In the South it hardly exists at all—indeed, in such States as Kentucky the people regard themselves as of direct British descent. But elsewhere there persists an unshaken tradition that Britain is a backward and reactionary country—the country, in other words, from which enlightened and progressive Young America broke away in the eighteenth century. The picture is still of a land ruled by and for the privileged and the few, in which merit has no opportunity to reap its reward or rise to the top. Only yesterday I heard a perfectly friendly American remark that in England the only way to success is to have the right father. One is constantly hearing, too, of aristocratic cliques gathering secretly in English country houses during week-ends and plotting to obstruct the flowing tide of democracy. Ask almost any American to tell you about the " Cliveden Set," and you will hear a story which will surprise you. It would also surprise the Cliveden Set, if such a set existed.

As for the British Empire, it was acquired, in the American view, by brutal wars of aggression and is maintained by plundering its oppressed inhabitants. The fact that no country in the world pays a penny of tribute to Britain is entirely unknown in America, and it would be a genuine surprise to the average American to be told that the British Empire practically abolished itself fifteen years ago when, under the Statute of Westminster, the Dominions became independent sovereign nations, with no obligation to stand by Britain at all, save that of loyalty to the British Crown.

We, on our part, are inclined to be equally and unreasonably critical of America. We, too, are a generation or so behindhand in our estimate of her point of view and way of life. We have got over the belief that cowboys and Red Indians roam up and down Broadway, but we are still inclined to regard America as a country of gangsters, bootleggers, and jazz-drummers. The fact that the vast majority of Americans are the most simple living, most domestic, most homekeeping people on earth is unrevealed to us.

We bicker, too, about things that do not matter, especially at a time like this. America derides our cooking, our cold houses, our antiquated coinage, above all our smug satisfaction with these things. We retaliate by criticising the American fondness for sensation and ballyhoo. Each of us is convinced that the other has no real sense of humour. Finally, we condemn one another's pronunciation of the English language. All of which is paltry and regrettable.

In other words, here are two great nations who would like to be cordial friends, but are held apart. Why? Three reasons suggest themselves. The first is that we parted in anger more than one hundred and fifty years ago; the second, that we are still to a certain extent blood relations, and everyone feels privileged to criticise his relatives more frankly than his friends; the third, that we enjoy the extremely doubtful blessing of a common language. It is not a blessing at all; it is a menace. If you are anxious to start trouble with anyone, it is much easier to do so with someone who understands what you are saying than with someone who does not.

Well, all this must stop, and probably will stop, or be sensibly eased, under the stress of common sacrifice. It is unlikely that we shall ever quite understand one another;

our respective national characteristics are too robust for that. But goodwill and tolerance can achieve miracles; so can common honesty of purpose. After all, we both believe in the same big things. Beside these, a few national fads and peculiarities are neither here nor there.

Since these words were written, our Prime Minister has delivered his address to Congress in Washington, in words which have rung round the world. In a speech of thirty minutes the foundations of Anglo-American friendship and of co-operation, upon a scale never yet achieved, have been well and truly laid. At least let us hope so.

XV

WASHINGTON, D.C.

MR. CHURCHILL has come and gone, and has left behind him an ineffaceable impression of broad vision, blunt candour, complete understanding of the American point of view, and high confidence in the future.

I write these words from Washington, which is still vibrating from the impact of our Prime Minister's personality. I have known this city well for more than twenty-five years, and have seen more than one swing of the international pendulum. I spent much time here during the latter part of the last war, and can remember delivering a lecture on Trench Warfare, in early 1917, before the United States entered the war, to a Washington audience which contained a considerable sprinkling of emissaries from the German Embassy, sent to catch me out in some statement which might be construed into a breach of neutrality. A few weeks later I formed one of the vast crowd which surged before the Capitol upon the April day when President Wilson declared war upon the Kaiser.

Washington is an unusual city, and in some ways unique. Like Canberra, its site was selected for sentimental reasons. No State in the Union would concede to any other the distinction of housing the Federal Capital. So a special miniature State was created to meet the situation. Washington stands in the District of Columbia, an isolated area of a few square miles, carved out of Maryland and Virginia, thus furnishing an acceptable compromise between North and South. Antipathy between North and South is not by any means extinct in America, even to-day, and never will be.

Unlike most capitals, Washington is laid out upon a calculated and symmetrical plan. It is about the size of Edinburgh. At the very centre stands the Capitol, a lofty, white-domed edifice which houses all Congressional activities. Above the Capitol by night and day flies the Stars and Stripes. At night both dome and flag are, or were, impressively floodlit. But not now. The capital of the Unites States is in the danger zone. Anti-aircraft guns are silhouetted against the sky high up on the roofs of Government offices. Soldiers with fixed bayonets guard the War Department.

From the Capitol grounds, like the spokes of a giant wheel, radiate a series of broad avenues, each named after a State of the Union. Even diminutive Rhode Island has its Avenue. Pennsylvania Avenue is the Whitehall of Washington. The White House bestrides it, and most of the Government Buildings abut upon it. The mile of its length from the White House to the Capitol furnishes a processional route for all great public functions.

These Avenues are of immense length, and penetrate far into the surrounding country. The new British Embassy lies upon the very outskirts of Washington, but is still within the city boundaries. Its address is 3100, Massachusetts Avenue. (The address of the United States Embassy in London, *per contra*, is 1 Grosvenor Square.) All of which serves to render Washington still further unique among American cities, for it is content with two dimensions—to expand laterally and not skyward. In Washington, to keep a business appointment you may have to travel two or three miles in a taxicab : in New York you stay where you are and shoot up to a seventieth floor in an express lift.

Upon this spoke-like system of avenues is superimposed the usual American gridiron of innumerable streets a block apart, crossing one another at right-angles. Wherever an Avenue cuts diagonally across one of these intersections, which it does perpetually, a roundabout or " Circle " is the result ; and as the streets of Washington are laid out upon an unusually broad and generous scale, and traffic can move swiftly, the risk to life and limb involved in the attempt to navigate one of these maelstroms successfully is even greater than in most American centres of population. The peril is heightened by the fact that Washington still sticks to that obsolete and unpredictable vehicle, the tramcar.

Washington, as befits a capital, is liberally endowed with monuments. George Washington and Abraham Lincoln each have their own. Lincoln's is a stately temple-like building beside the waters of the Potomac River, on the other bank of which lies the National Cemetery of Arlington and the tomb of the Unknown Soldier. (It is noticeable that he is described as a soldier and not as a warrior, thus excluding the possibility of his being a sailor or marine.) George Washington has a soaring obelisk, resembling a giant Cleopatra's needle. It is some hundreds of feet high, and you may ascend in a lift to the top for a glorious view of the surrounding country.

And there are statues innumerable. Most of them appear to be generals. Grant, Sherman, Sheridan, Andrew Jackson, they are all there. So is Lafayette, the French aristocratic free-lance who came to the aid of the American Colonies during the War of Independence. In the opposite corner of the same green square stands Von Steuben, a stumpy Prussian, once the Aide-de-Camp of Frederick the Great, who was sent over during the same period, to 'inculcate military discipline into the " embattled farmers." He did most of the spadework, while Lafayette did most of the posturing. He is entirely forgotten now.

Washington possesses but one industry. The seat of American trade and finance is New York City ; Washington concerns itself only with politics and diplomacy. In London and Paris the arts of diplomacy are discreetly buried amid the activities of millions of laymen : in Washington they stick out a yard in every direction. Mark Twain once observed long ago that upon the Continent of Europe you cannot throw a brick anywhere without crippling a king. You may say with somewhat greater truth that in Washington you can, or could, hardly throw a stone anywhere without breaking the window of an Embassy or Legation. If you dined out in the easy-going, gossipy Washington of peace-time, you had to be prepared to meet half a dozen nationalities, and utter a few polite conventional phrases in almost any tongue, from Portuguese to Polish.

But those pleasant polyglot days are over. Washington now speaks but one language, Anglo-Saxon. British Missions—Naval, Military, R.A.F.—are here in force, some of them a bequest from Mr. Churchill's visit, and confer daily with their American opposite numbers. Geographically, Washington is well placed to be the scene of such conferences. Indeed, most Americans would like to see something in the nature of an Allied

General Headquarters established here. London, they say, is too near the battle-line. It is neither convenient nor helpful to discuss measures of broad strategy during an air-raid or attempted invasion. Moreover, the presence of a Supreme War Council in Washington, handling the problems of every front, would prevent Americans from regarding the war—and millions of them still do—as a single issue between America and Japan.

There is much to be said to this point of view, but for the present, at any rate, there is more to be said on the other side. Britain is undoubtedly the predominant partner in the Allied cause, and British public servants have had more than two years' active experience both of strategy and production. In Britain, too, we are solid. We have no Labour troubles, and we possess what amounts to a National Government. We criticise it freely, but nobody really wants to get rid of it, least of all of its leader. In Washington party politics still hold sway. The President is bitterly criticised in many quarters. We are told that he is not the man to win the war. He is too sanguine, too superficial, too much of a day-to-day opportunist. Isolationism, too, is by no means dead. There are still those who would rather score party points than concentrate on victory.

Above all, the present atmosphere of Washington itself is entirely adverse to anything like calm deliberation or ordered planning. The city is full to overflowing, with officials, delegates, place-seekers and commentators. It is almost impossible to get a room or bed, or for that matter, a seat upon the trains or planes proceeding thereto. New departments are springing up everywhere : it is said that there are eighty-five thousand stenographers in Washington to-day. The public services are over-taxed : the only reply one ever receives over the telephone seems to be "Line busy." A ribald American friend informed me to-day that Washington is the only madhouse in existence run entirely by its inmates. Anyhow, amid such turmoil it is impossible to take long views about anything, or to keep those views secret.

All this has a familiar ring for us, and we cannot but sympathise. We know that presently order will emerge from confusion, and the mighty machine begin to function. And it may be that in a year's time, as our various battle fronts become more clearly defined and our points of attack more plainly indicated, the Federal Capital of the United States, situated midway between the battle-fronts of the Atlantic and the Pacific, may well furnish the Allied council chamber in which our final and victorious plans will be formulated.

XVI

OUR NAVAL AMBASSADORS

I HAVE just returned from a visit to the great American Navy Yard at Brooklyn. Almost immediately above it towers the mighty Brooklyn Bridge which spans the so-called East River and joins Manhattan to Long Island. The Yard itself is enclosed upon three sides by the usual lofty dockyard wall, and no one passes through its gates to-day who is not most thoroughly authenticated.

The scene within those walls at this moment can be imagined. Ships building, ships refitting, ships repairing. Battered, mangled ships being born anew. New buildings going up, greater docks being dug; the thud of pile-drivers, the clatter of rivetting machinery, the blinding flame of the acetylene welders. Motor-trolleys swiftly conveying workmen to some fresh job in a distant corner. Here and there a slogan chalked up—" Remember Pearl Harbour ! "

But to British eyes the most interesting feature must be the British ships. Here close by us in a dry-dock rests —if the term can be applied to such a turmoil of activity— a long, lean British light cruiser. She looks dingy and unkempt ; she has been stripped of all her fittings ; her decks are a writhing snare of electric cables conveying power to the repairing machinery. Upon her starboard side, forward of the engine-room, is a gaping wound, inflicted by an Axis torpedo. Despite that wound she has made her way across the winter Atlantic under her own steam, and now, in this friendly haven, is being rendered trim and right again by hundreds of willing and most efficient American hands, working in shifts all round the clock, for further distinguished service.

This morning her crew, to their mild surprise, read in the newspaper an enemy communiqué to the effect that their ship was now lying at the bottom of the sea somewhere off Tobruk, dispatched thither by three well-directed torpedoes.

" There was only one torpedo," commented her Commander dryly, as I returned the cutting to him, " and it dispatched us to Brooklyn. Otherwise the statement is substantially correct. Come on board and have a look round."

" I never find myself in a ship of war," I remarked, removing my hand from a hot steam-pipe which I had mistakenly imagined to be a hand-rail—" always as full of machinery as the inside of a watch—without wondering where on earth they contrive to put the crew. How many men do you carry ? "

" Normally, about five hundred. At least, that's what

she's designed for. But on war service you usually find
yourself with an extra hundred on your hands." The
Commander opened a steel door and showed me what
looked like a short section of a passage. It was bare
and unoccupied, except for a man on his hands and knees
apparently shampooing the deck with a species of electric
flat-iron, which purred and emitted a shower of sparks.
" This is the Chief Petty Officers' Mess—twenty-five of
them. A bit crowded, but they manage. Of course
they're seldom all there at the same time. And we
even find room on board for recreational space. Look
in here ! "

We were in another closed-in passage now, much longer
and surprisingly wide, lit by port-holes. " Here is where
the men come and sit about in their spare time," said the
Commander. " They have a bar, and the place is just
long enough to be used as a cinema. We get some quite
good films."

Well, the crew of the *Golden Hind* had no cinema shows.
Otherwise, so far as elbow-room is concerned, Drake's
men and Cunningham's men seem still to have a good
deal in common.

Meanwhile, with the ship lying stripped and uninhabit-
able—the Commander's office is the only cabin in use—
officers and men are housed ashore. And here is something to note and a question to ask—and a good deal of
naval co-operation and efficiency hangs on the answer.
The number of British naval vessels refitted and repaired
in this and other yards up and down the American seaboard runs by this time into hundreds, and the men who
have been loosed ashore during the period of waiting,
into thousands. How have they been received and treated,
and how have they responded ?

In this vitally important connexion let us remember
two things. The first is that British sailors, although

they find themselves entirely at home in most foreign ports, are strangers in America. British naval vessels are not in the habit of calling at American ports, except upon some rare visit of ceremony. Moreover, from the point of view of Jack ashore for a day's enjoyment, so far as his resources will permit, the rate of exchange in the United States to-day is sorely against Jack. Moreover, prices have soared to the usual war-time level.

Well, America has taken care of all that. The kindness and hospitality lavished upon our men from the sea has exceeded even the usual American scale, and that is saying something. The Union Jack Club, endowed mainly with American money and situated, not in some drab and uninspiring location near the Navy Yard, but within a stone's throw of that Mecca to which all New York visitors of whatever degree immediately gravitate—Times Square, which is the equivalent of our Piccadilly Circus or Leicester Square—stands open to all our men in uniform. Here you will receive a warm welcome from friendly ladies, obtain an excellent meal at nominal rates, with liquid refreshment upon even more reasonable terms. There is a generous supply of free theatre and cinema tickets. You may even go to a dance if you prefer it, and many do.

Hospitality is not limited to official or impersonal effort. At least two well-known New York Clubs throw open their premises once a week to a batch—twenty or so—of British sailors. The members entertain these guests in the Club dining-room, and then dispatch them to " a show."

We maintain in New York and other American bases a British Naval Liaison Officer, whose duty it is to get into immediate touch with incoming British crews, most of them sorely in need of rest and recreation, and introduce them to American hospitality.

That hospitality is everywhere and instantly forth-coming. For instance, British sailors are frequently invited to spend Christmas or a week-end in an American home, as one of the family. It is easy to picture the disastrous situation if all this kindness were to be un-appreciated or abused. It could do more harm to the Allied cause than Goebbels and all his minions working overtime. But it is very much appreciated, and our sailors gratefully and punctiliously signify the fact; which is proved by the number of letters received by our ship's officers from hosts and hostesses, commending the im-peccable behaviour of their guests and asking for more.

Our officers and men are also meeting and mingling with their opposite numbers in the American Navy. They may or may not be conscious of the responsibility which rests upon them in this respect, but there is no doubting the success with which they are carrying it out.

And this brings us to the second point. The whole future of the world, both to-day and to-morrow, rests upon Anglo-American accord. That accord never has been—and never will be—easy of achievement. Despite the similarity of our outlook, laws, and traditions, tem-peramentally we are poles apart.

The American is forthcoming, impulsive, demonstrative. The Englishman is constrained, awkward, slow to make friends. Consequently many Americans regard the English as being unsociable and stuck-up. Americans too, are almost aggressively patriotic. They not only regard themselves as the greatest nation on earth and the leaders of the world, but are fond of impressing that belief upon themselves and their friends and neighbours. Of course we British hold a similar high opinion of ourselves. The difference is that we are quietly and irritatingly complacent about it, while the American, as he himself will readily confess to you, likes to make the Eagle scream.

American exuberance is not due to conceit. The cause is entirely different. America is a comparatively young member of the comity of nations, and she feels, not without reason, that the older countries are inclined to be a little patronising towards her, despite her overwhelming strength and prestige. She is conscious, as a famous American once said, of " a certain condescension in foreigners," and that galls an American to the roots of his being. So he overstates his case and overplays his hand, partly to impress the foreigner, and partly to satisfy his own legitimate pride in the noble heritage he has built up.

In other words, the Americans are a people peculiarly sensitive to criticism or patronage, especially from the British. The British character, with its peculiar blend of easy-going tolerance and blind self-satisfaction, is almost impervious to criticism from any quarter.

That is why the antics of some of our back-bench politicians at home seem, especially to British observers here in America, to pass the bounds of human understanding.

Within the past few weeks, after discussions which must have called for the exercise of an infinity of tact and goodwill on either side, the American people have accepted a British Commander-in-Chief, Sir Archibald Wavell, over the whole of the operations in the South-western Pacific. A few months ago the idea of American sailors, soldiers, marines and airmen serving under a foreign commander, especially a British commander, would, to any one with the slightest knowledge of Anglo-American history and relations during the past century and a half, been unthinkable. Yet this thing has happened. America has made the gesture, and made it with the best of grace.

And yet during a discussion in the House of Commons which covered this historic event, one member appears to have risen in his place to lament the fact that England was being reduced to the position of an American outpost in Europe—" an American Heligoland "—while another, not to be outdone in tact and international courtesy, protested against British sailors being put under the orders of an American Admiral.

The authors of these helpful utterances are, of course, well known to the House of Commons, and their views are rated at their proper value. It is doubtful if their speeches were even reported in the British Press. But in America they were reported in full, with appropriate headlines, and the further westward the views travelled, the bigger the headlines and the more caustic the comments. In fact, the anti-British brigade have had the time of their lives.

Speech being free, there is presumably no means of muzzling these patriots of ours, except perhaps through the good sense of their constituents ; but it seems unfortunate that the success of an historic mission of goodwill and co-operation recently undertaken by our Prime Minister should be jeopardised by ill-informed and ill-mannered comment of this kind.

This brings us back to our men in American ports. Here, indeed, is happy contrast. British and American sailors by the thousand, wherever they meet, are determined upon just one thing, and that is to pull together and beat Hitler. Unlike our back-bench friends, they are realists and men of the world. Upon their joint shoulders to-day rests the safety of the Seven Seas, which means the safety of civilisation ; and they know it. So they go forward, united.

XVII

CONGRESS IN SESSION

I HAVE just spent a highly interesting day in the Capitol at Washington, observing the methods by which Congress conducts the legislative business of the United States, and making certain inevitable comparisons.

Of course there must be a similarity in all parliamentary procedure, for most national democratic assemblies conform in part to the ancient pattern of the Mother of Parliaments. In the House of Representatives at Washington the Chairman is called Mr. Speaker, although, as in our House of Commons, he is the most taciturn member present, and all speeches are nominally addressed to him. Then there is the Mace—last relic and reminder of British rule—and unless and until the Mace is in place the House is not in session. Personnel, too, is recruited upon much the same lines as our own : the more thickly populated an electoral district, the larger the number of members which it returns.

Then there is the deportment and demeanour of the members themselves. In this respect legislators do not seem to vary much as a class ; except at rare intervals they display not the slightest interest in the remarks of the gentleman who is in possession of the floor of the House. They chatter to one another, they read letters, they rustle papers, they doze, or they stroll in and out of ever-swinging doors—more frequently out than in. The only persons present who behave with complete propriety are the visitors in the gallery, who being technically invisible, must not betray their presence either by movement or demonstration.

But there the resemblance ceases. Our House of Commons is, or, alas ! was, all Gothic and stately within.

It was dimly lit and inclined to be stuffy. As a debating chamber it was so arranged that a minister speaking from the front bench was more or less inaudible to his own followers, who were grouped behind him. Indeed, he could not turn anywhere without presenting his back to somebody, and he was not assisted by the fact that the acoustics of the chamber were, and probably will be, atrocious. Finally, its dimensions were such that only about two-thirds of the members could find seats.

Then there is tradition—the tradition of centuries. There is Mr. Speaker himself, with his knee-breeches, full-bottomed wig and flowing robes, and the solemn pageantry of his daily entrance and exit. There are various customs and precedents, some of which have ceased to have any meaning or necessity, but are still lovingly cherished. A member wishing to intervene in a debate at a certain and particular stage can only do so sitting down and wearing his or, quite frequently, somebody else's hat. There is a red line marked on the floor at the end of the gangway beyond which a member may not step while speaking, lest in the heat of debate he should be tempted to draw his sword upon his opponent.

This, as may be imagined, is neither the atmosphere nor the tradition of the House of Representatives in Washington. The chamber itself looks more like a modern concert hall, with its light-coloured walls, glass roof, surrounding galleries, and innumerable doors with an attendant at each. Mr. Speaker's dais, a white marble three-decker, stands half-way along one of the side walls, with the members facing it in a semicircle composed of six wedge-shaped blocks of seats (as in the House of Representatives at Delhi) each tapering to a blunt point at the foot of the dais.

A member wishing to address the House at length takes his stand at a lectern, with his back to Mr. Speaker. He usually reads his manuscript into a microphone—and audiences the world over know to their cost that over the microphone most voices and all political speeches sound very much alike. Moreover, such members of Congress as I heard seemed to make little attempt to dramatise their speeches. They just went ahead without pause, or without waiting as a rule for the reaction of their audience. But there was an explanation for this, as I was to realise.

This brings us to an item of Congressional procedure quite unknown to our House of Commons. If a member of Congress proposes to deliver what he regards as a really momentous speech—a speech which, in his opinion, demands a worthy audience—he has the right to demand that the roll of the House shall be called. Possibly he makes that demand himself, but more usually it is made upon his behalf by an accommodating friend. Members answer to their names, and absentees are summoned. The roll is then called a second time, and if enough members to form a quorum of more than half the House have now assembled, the orator proceeds to his task. If necessary, the roll can be called a third time; but usually twice is enough.

The most obvious objection to this custom is that it wastes time. To call the roll twice takes forty minutes. But among the legislatures of the world Congress enjoys no monopoly of time-wasting. The average period occupied by our own Members of Parliament in tramping through a division lobby is a quarter of an hour; so that three House of Commons divisions are equal, or more than equal, to a Congress roll-call. Members of Congress, by the way, vote from their seats, calling aye or no in answer to their names.

In some American State Legislature elaborate mechanical voting devices are employed. At Baton Rouge, State

Capital of Louisiana, upon a huge board set up on the wall of the Senate behind the Chairman's seat is a complete list of all the Senators' names. When it comes to voting, a member merely presses one of two buttons beside his desk, and his vote is immediately indicated by a green or red light beside his name on the board ; so the verdict of the House is plain to see in a few moments.

A duplicate of this board is set up in the Governor's private office close by, from which that functionary can take note of the course of the voting, and incidentally of the orthodoxy of his followers. The late lamented Huey Long is said to have kept an eagle eye upon this board, and when a light showed red amid a dutiful forest of green, the backslider speedily found himself on the carpet, and, in extreme cases, on the spot.

One objection to the Congress roll-call device for conscripting an audience is that it opens the door too widely to the parliamentary bore. In our own House of Commons the uprising of one of the species is merely a signal for the House to empty ; in Congress it is a compulsory summons to the House to assemble. But a member of Congress need not remain after he has answered to his name ; and in any case the privilege of the roll-call is seldom abused, because the rules of the House provide a simple and ingenious alternative. It is this :

Whenever an unimportant private member addresses the House, whether in Congress or Commons, we must bear in mind all the time that he is not addressing his fellow members at all. He is merely calling the attention of his own constituents, in some remote American State or English county, to the zeal, industry and importance of their representative. In England, though the London press will probably ignore it altogether, his speech will be reported verbatim in the local paper, which is all he wants. The fact that it was delivered to empty benches is unrevealed. The only sufferer is the British Government, which has lost an hour of parliamentary time.

They order these things better in America. Upon the day of my visit to Congress, the House of Representatives was called upon to approve the Daylight Saving Bill, which puts the clock forward an hour all the year round, as with us. The result was a foregone conclusion; but certain members representing rural and agricultural States were in duty bound to protest. A member rose and claimed the indulgence of the House "for the space of one minute." This being granted, he advanced to the microphone burdened with a considerable manuscript, and began an impassioned oration. At the end of the allotted minute the hammer came down sharply. The orator broke off, turned and handed his manuscript to the clerk at the table, and resumed his seat. He had achieved his end: the speech would appear next day, in full in the *Congressional Record*, thoughtfully interspersed with "Cheers," "Laughter," and "Applause," and his reputation among his constituents for faithful and forthright service would be enhanced, all at the cost of sixty seconds of Congressional time. One cannot help feeling that this scheme should be submitted to our own Committee on Parliamentary Procedure forthwith. It would be adopted by acclamation.

But the most striking contrast between the House of Commons and the House of Representatives is the apparent lack of leadership in the latter. There is no Prime Minister, no Leader of the Opposition, no Front Bench at all. This is largely because practically all official initiative in America is vested in the President. The only acknowledged authorities in the House are the Majority Leader and the Minority Leader, each of whom is not much more than a party whip. The spadework of legislation is done by a series of Standing Committees—the Foreign Affairs

Committee, the Military Affairs Committee, and countless others—each with its own President, which draft the necessary bills for the consideration of Congress.

Above all, there is no Question Time in Congress, no heckling of Ministers—a consummation which must be greeted by our own Front Bench with a sigh of envy. The fact is, there are no Ministers there to heckle. American Cabinets are not greatly concerned with conciliating public opinion. With us it is different. A keenly-pointed question, and a tactless or bungled answer may lead to a motion for the adjournment of the House, the result of which may be a ministerial defeat and the resignation of the Government, all within the space of a few hours. But Congress is threatened with no such sudden calamity ; it is elected for a term of years, and so are its responsible officials. Ambushes mean nothing to these.

It remains to be added that Congressmen are more pampered than with us. Each receives a salary of ten thousand dollars a year, and is also given a suite of offices in a spacious building close by. It has to be spacious, for there are five hundred and thiry-five Congressmen. The Senate, too, has its own Office Building, and each building is connected with the Capitol by a subway. Senators enjoy the added privilege of a miniature underground electric train to convey them to and from their labours.

Of the Senate itself, it is sufficient to say that it is the House of Representatives in miniature. There are ninety-six members, two from each State, and they are presided over by the Vice-President of the United States. They sit each at a desk instead of on a bench, and their debates are consequently more intimate and conversational. The microphone is not employed, and this gives far more opportunity to character and personality.

Such, then, are a few of the differences in tradition and

procedure between the two greatest Legislatures in the world, as they appear to the casual visitor. Speech and opinion are free and untrammelled in both, and the humblest can aspire to their highest offices, as our joint histories have good and grateful cause to remember. That is all that matters, especially in these days, when we need all the good men we can get.

XVIII

BILLIONS OF BUCKS

THE American people are settling down to war, a war which for the first time in their history as a sovereign nation threatens their actual hearths and homes—or, you might say, their radiators and skyscrapers—and they are making discoveries, mostly disagreeable, which have long been familiar to ourselves.

The first is that in total war the industrial resources of an entire country must be converted, as nearly over-night as possible, to the production of warlike material; and in the case of America this material must suffice not merely for America's needs but for many of those of her hard-pressed Allies as well.

The President's State of the Union speech, recently delivered, certainly does not blink this fact. It puts forward a programme of effort and expenditure which has fairly staggered the world, and must be the cause of some hard thinking in Berlin and Tokyo.

The estimated national income of the United States is about a hundred thousand million dollars a year. These, of course, are astronomical figures so far as ordinary human comprehension is concerned, but the simple and essential point to observe is that whereas America so far has only been spending fifteen per cent. of that income upon warlike preparation, she now proposes to spend over sixty per cent. To put it another way, America during 1942 is going to spend roughly three times as much per day upon the war as we are spending in Britain. Since the population of the United States is three times the size of our own, this gives each of us approximately an equal share of the burden.

This means that American incomes of every grade will now be taxed to the level of our own—possibly higher, because an American frequently has to pay both State and Federal taxes out of one income—and the average American will find himself deprived, in increasing measure, of innumerable everyday commodities which he has come to regard as automatic adjuncts to his comfortable standard of living. For instance, no more motor-cars are to be manufactured, and in a country where no one walks when he can ride, and practically every working man arrives at his job in his own jalopy—the jalopy is the lineal decendant of the Tin Lizzie—the privation is going to be felt far more widely and keenly than with us. Already tyres have been rationed, and are becoming as hard to obtain as eggs and oranges elsewhere. Other shortages and further rationing will occur as the country settles down to its revised scale of living. As I write, all railway fares have been raised ten per cent., and the consumption of sugar is to be limited. In other words, this land of comfort and plenty is about to undergo, for the first time in eighty years, the hard pinch of real war conditions. The pinch during the last war was comparatively light.

Not that there is a word of complaint or repining to be heard. Indeed, the American citizen has for long felt uneasily conscious that he is living in plenty while the world is starving; and with the impulsive generosity of his race he almost welcomes the opportunity to share in some measure the privations of his friends.

The President's programme of production for the present year is prodigious. It provides for the manufacture of sixty thousand aircraft, forty-five thousand tanks, thirty-five thousand anti-aircraft guns, and eight million tons of merchant shipping. In 1943 it is expected that production of all this equipment, except ships, will be doubled. Here, again, are figures before which human imagination totters.

But whereas the country is enthusiastically at one upon the matter of expenditure, there are two very definite attitudes of mind upon the question of production. The majority shout: " Hooray for Uncle Sam; he has done it again ! " (Note that they say " has done it," and not " will do it.") Americans love the grand scale; they revel in big figures and the very sound of the word billions. To us a billion is a million million, which renders infrequent our employment of the term in our everyday arithmetic; but to Americans it is a thousand million, which, especially when applied to dollars, makes it possible to employ it in these days with comparative frequency and impressive effect.

Thoughtful Americans, on the other hand—and there are some very thoughtful people in America to-day—decline to be dazzled by this vision of billions. They are mistrustful of short-lived enthusiasm and of the American tendency to accept promise for performance and the will for the deed. Some of them remember the last war and the huge appropriations which were made by President Wilson's Government for aircraft and heavy guns. These were hailed at the time with jubilant acclaim, yet when the Armistice came in 1918 the American Expeditionary Force were still compelled to rely very largely upon aircraft

and heavy guns of French and British design and manufacture. "That must not happen this time," they say.

And there is need to say it, for the American preparedness
campaign has been hampered from the start by its own
intensity. Every department has been trying to fulfil its
own requirements at the highest possible speed, without
any particular regard for the needs or feelings of other
departments. The result has been confusion and wasteful
competition. There has been a wild scramble for what
are known as priorities. Each of the fighting services
wants steel for tanks, guns and ships. Each of them
has been in the habit, through its Quartermaster-General
or equivalent official, of going direct to the manufacturer
for this, clamouring for immediate delivery and sometimes
doubling the size of the order in the hope of getting at
least something. The result has been an automatic increase in the price of steel and inevitable delay in delivery.
If these orders had been submitted through a responsible
Ministry of Supply they could have been graded according
to urgency and distributed in such a way and over such an
interval of time as to ensure a steady flow of production
and an even price level. We ourselves in Britain have
long learned this lesson by the road of trial and error.
Now America has recognised its importance, and everybody is anxious to see the matter regularised; but until
recently nobody seems to have had the authority to do
it. That was one of the first things which Mr Churchill's
advisory experts discovered when they visited Washington
a few weeks ago.

And, therefore, the most momentous and far-reaching
step, or rather stride, taken by President Roosevelt since
the entry of the United States into the war is the appointment of Mr. Donald Nelson as Director-General of Production, at the head of the new War Production Board,
which will entirely supersede a body known as the Office

of Production Management, in which authority and initiative were so subdivided as to render it both unwieldy and ineffective.

Mr. Nelson begins with the advantage of having no political commitments to hamper him. He is, or was, head of the great mail-order firm of Sears, Roebuck, which means that he understands the problems of purchase and distribution as few other men even in America. You might compare him in experience and ability with our own Lord Woolton, and his powers will be even greater. All applications for production material must pass through him, and his word is final.

Mr. Nelson can and will do valuable work in another direction. Washington to-day is congested by hordes of manufacturers or their agents, soliciting orders or seeking direction regarding orders already lodged. Much valuable time is consumed by the very journeys of these petitioners between the capital and their own home district, sometimes over thousands of miles. Mr. Nelson is meeting this difficulty by a policy of decentralisation. He will establish trusty agents in various parts of the country to deal with applications locally, referring back to himself as occasion arises.

He will also, it is hoped and expected, get rid of some of the so-called dollar-a-year men. An extremely severe report, the Truman Report, upon the activities of some of these altruists has just been issued by a Special Committee of the Senate. A dollar-a-year man is a business man who, for a nominal annual salary of one dollar, puts his own business entirely aside for the duration and devotes himself to the service of the State. In many cases, the Truman Report asserts, this sacrifice is more apparent than real, for the gentleman in question frequently employs his official knowledge and position to secure favourable contracts and priorities for his own firm.

Mr. Nelson is surrounded by a strong board of advisers. It contains the Vice-President of the United States, and such men as the Secretary of the Navy, Mr. Knox, and that remarkable person, Mr. Knudson, who until recently had been occupying the conspicuous but uncomfortable position of a square peg in a round hole at the head of the now defunct Office of Production Management. He is no administrator, but he possesses one of the best engineering and mechanical brains in the country. He knows as much about motor-cars as Lord Nuffield himself, and has had a very similar history. Henceforth he will be free to roam at will and give practical advice regarding the adaptation of commercial machinery to war-like requirements. He will be in his element.

So much, then, for the vigorous and heartening measures now in hand throughout the United States for the forging of the decisive war-weapon of the present world struggle : the weapon of intensive production. Many and hazardous are the difficulties which still lie ahead. The great and powerful motor-car industry is inclined to be obstructive over the question of the complete conversion of its plant to warlike use. It predicts heavy unemployment during the transition stage. Then there is the labour question. The two rival organisations—the American Federation of Labor and the Congress of Industrial Organisations—are jointly considering a scheme of amalgamation, ostensibly for the furtherance of war effort. Their deliberations so far have mainly been distinguished by the resolute determination of either side to swallow the other. There is the menace of sabotage, always considerable in a country of vast size and mixed population. Nearly thirty per cent. of the population of certain American cities is European by birth and sentiment. So far there has been a gratifying freedom from serious damage ; it is agreed that the Federal Board of Intelligence are doing a " swell job " in this respect.

So here America stands to-day, with billions of bucks to spend and a colossal programme of production to spend it on. And if America can keep her feet on the ground and see to it that this time there is no confusion between desire and performance, all will be well, triumphantly well.

Even if one-half of this year's programme is carried out it will be something, and more than something, the average American considers. And he is right.

XIX

THE SELECTEES

ALL able-bodied American citizens to-day between the ages of twenty-one and forty-five are liable for military service, under what is known as the Selective Draft. Each man has a draft number, which is a kind of military lottery-ticket with the man himself as the prize. Whenever—and if ever—his number emerges from the lottery-wheel, he must report for duty forthwith. It does not follow that he will have to serve. He may be " deferred " as a man with a family to support, or "exempted " as being under the required physical standard. Deferment and exemption are frequent because, with a reservoir of one hundred and thirty millions at his disposal, Uncle Sam can afford to pick and choose to an extent unknown in our heavily committed little island.

The usual seasonable gibes are being bandied upon the subject. The flow of humour inseparable from the income-tax evasion has now received military reinforcement. " Please, Colonel," a conscientious recruit is depicted as asking the chairman of his Draft Board, " can I use the same baby for draft deferment as I used for tax-remission ? "

However, the remaining millions who are unhampered by babies or other responsibilities, speedily find themselves in the United States Army, where they are called Selectees. I have just been spending a day with several thousands of them.

The scene of our encounter is a great camp in one of the Eastern States—a country of rolling plain, sandy soil, and scattered pine-woods, pleasantly reminiscent of our own familiar Aldershot. The sun is glittering in a cloudless sky, and the thermometer marks several degrees of frost. The great majority of the Selectees are undergoing their training in the more clement South. Only one Division is stationed here; but this particular camp serves more than one purpose, as we shall see. An important point is that it is served by two lines of railway.

Originally a regular and permanent military "post" of modest dimensions, the camp now spreads far and wide, absorbing farms and country estates over many thousands of acres. Some of these properties had deep roots: the title-deeds of one farm dated back to King George the Second of England. Now it has been requisitioned in aid of another King George of England.

Soldiers are training in all directions, and like ours their warfare is mainly mechanical. There are tanks, motor-lorries, and heavy guns drawn by tractors. There are artillery ranges and machine-gun ranges and miniature ranges and combat areas. Considerable distances have to be covered, and with all possible speed. For these a jeep is usually employed. A jeep is something like our platoon-truck, only smaller and of an indescribable toughness. It is a sort of iron box upon four wheels, and is propelled by all four of them; which means that it can face almost any gradient and is quite independent of anything in the shape of a beaten path. A journey in a jeep, o'er crag and torrent, moor and fen, is an experience to be remembered, especially by an ageing veteran of the last war. Jeeps are probably careering round Northern Ireland by this time.*

But the chief importance of Camp X is as a Reception Centre, so-called. Here the new arrivals are put through a course of conversion from civilian to soldier so swift, so intensive, so completely standardised as to arouse in the spectator a vivid memory of a visit once paid, and a day once spent, in the stockyards and packing plants of Chicago. In other words, our draftees are fed in at one end of the machine to emerge, after a variety of unusual experiences, clothed, equipped, and grounded in the rudiments of their new profession at the other. The only difference is that whereas a Chicago machine can carry a sausage through all stages of its manufacture in a few hours, it takes five days to convert a Draftee into a Buck Private.

Here is the most lately arrived contingent, waiting outside the first of a series of long Army huts. All as yet are in civilian clothing, which ranges from the neat business suit of the bank clerk to the denim overall of the garage-hand. One sturdy young man is wearing a jersey upon which is embroidered in staring letters the surprising legend : " Southern Methodist Mustangs "—presumably a College football team.

As already noted, this assemblage are only here for five days, but their experiences during that period will be close-packed. Each man will be inoculated against smallpox, enteric, and tetanus. Some of us can remember the discomfort attending these operations ; but to-day, one is informed, all these injections can be administered at once and without producing any uncomfortable re-action. He will receive instruction in the Articles of War and Sex Morality. He will be made acquainted with Army rationing and barrack-room beds. He will learn to stand in line and perform simple drill movements. He

* I note that they are in London too.

will then be despatched to a Replacement Training Camp for thirteen weeks. After that he may find himself in almost any part of the habitable globe, from Iceland to Australia.

Such contingents as this are arriving at and departing from this particular Reception Centre at the rate of five hundred a day. Let Berlin and Tokyo multiply that figure by the number of Reception Centres throughout the length and breadth of this great land, and then sit back and think.

Our present party are assembled for the first day of what we will call their Chicago treatment. They file into the first of the huts, where each man presently finds himself seated at a small table, at which a slick N.C.O. registers his name, age, weight, occupation, and other details, for his card-index. A glance over a couple of shoulders reveals the occupations of the two nearest draftees as those of *Garbage-man* and *Biologist* respectively. Uncle Sam throws a wide net. Incidentally one recalls that long ago and far away, the first three twenty-year-olds to register at a certain enrolment station under our brand-new Militia Scheme in 1939 in England, were the son of a duke, a bricklayer's labourer, and an undertaker's assistant.

All the index cards are of uniform size and pattern. There are a number of holes punched along the top of each, each hole denoting a different trade or profession. When the cards are all filed together, standing on edge in a drawer, the holes will form a series of little tunnels, through which thin metal rods pass. These are a labour-saving device. Supposing there should be a call for twenty truck-drivers, there is no need to examine each card in detail. By a simple manipulation of one of the rods, all the truck-driver cards are made to drop out of the file, and a selection can be made in a moment.

Now the party proceeds to the second hut, for an intelligence test, which consists in writing the answers to a hundred and fifteen carefully graded questions. The early questions are quite elementary—some simple arithmetical calculation, perhaps, or test of a man's power of observation. "What is the next number in the series 3-6-9?" Or, "How many legs has a fly?" The later questions are more advanced, and are calculated to test a man's educational standard, readiness of perception, and fitness for this or that technical branch. Very often three or four alternative answers are supplied with the question itself, and the examinee merely has to strike out those which he regards as incorrect. This standardises and simplifies the labour of those who scrutinise the papers, which they do with remarkable speed. Before a man leaves this hut he knows the result of the examination and his own particular category.

Special provision is made for the illiterate and backward. To exclude such from their country's service *en bloc* might be to lose some soldier of promise who has merely lacked educational opportunity. Besides, a man may be extremely useful with his hands who has no head to speak of.

Here is such an individual—a negro in this case—undergoing his first experience in the exercise of his intelligence. He is sitting at a desk, contemplating with a perplexed frown a large cube of wood set upon a table a few feet away. He can see that the cube is composed of a number of smaller cubes of uniform size. His problem is to calculate how many small cubes the large cube contains, given that each face of the large cube shows nine small cubes. Obviously the calculation is beyond him, so he is tackling the problem in his own way, by making a drawing of the cube—a remarkably neat one, incidentally—shading in the small cubes one by one, and then counting up the result on his fingers. His puzzled frown is due to the fact that he cannot figure how many small cubes are hidden from sight inside the large one. Let us hope he will make a successful shot.

We proceed to the next hut. Here the men receive a brief, concise lecture upon their obligations and rights as soldiers. Each of them is also asked whether he wishes to accept the Army scheme of life insurance. The scheme is optional, because many draftees are men of substance, and have no need of State aid.

The next step is a brief medical inspection, in case any of the new arrivals should be suffering from any temporary ailment unfitting him for immediate service. All were overhauled for organic defects upon registration, and before being posted to the Army at all. It would be interesting to know what percentage of these men have been passed fit for active service. In the case of our own young Militiamen, the percentage in the original batch was ninety-three, an extraordinarily high level, and a real tribute to the war-babies of 1919, which they actually were.

The day is wearing on, and now at long last comes the beginning of our draftee's visible transformation into a soldier. He is about to shed his variegated civilian plumage and assume the protective colouring of khaki. The process is gradual and progressive, still on the Chicago model.

He begins by receiving a stout canvas bag, which in future will house the whole of his worldly possessions. It is already furnished with a knife, fork, spoon, and such standard toilet articles as a toothbrush. Thereafter he joins a long line of fellow draftees filing slowly past busy sergeants in charge of mechanical contrivances which measure each man for shoes, trousers, tunic and cap. Then, with a slip of paper in his hand recording all his bodily dimensions, he presents himself at a series of counters in the ultimate hut, and is issued, step by step, with his new articles of attire. At each counter he discards a civilian garment and invests himself in corresponding raiment of khaki. It is a strange, piebald procession, and varies in hue and pattern all along the line.

Last of all come shoes. To an American both boots and shoes are just shoes; but these really are shoes, or to be quite correct, low shoes. They are rubber-soled, heavily grooved, and resemble the type favoured by the modern golfer, or London policeman. On the march this will be a silent army in comparison with our own hob-nailed clumpers. That has been noted already: the inhabitants of Northern Ireland are reported as having been particularly impressed by the noiseless progress of the American troops over the cobble-stones of Ulster. As soon as a man's new shoes are fitted, he is made to stand for a given time with a bucket in his hand containing a quantity of sand equivalent to the exact weight of his rifle and equipment. This is a thoughtful precaution, for shoes which are perfectly comfortable upon first acquaintance can become torture to a man in full marching order. If the bucket of sand produces any such symptoms, the sufferer is put back for a larger pair.

All is over at last, and our selectee is free to return to the outer air. Fixed in the wall of the hut, beside the door through which he is about to emerge, he comes face to face with a full-length mirror, in which is reflected a figure in the uniform of the United States Army—his first vision of himself as a soldier of Uncle Sam. He takes a full breath, straightens his civilian back, squares his shoulders, and marches proudly forth into the winter sunshine, to adventures unknown and unpredictable.

XX

WAR NEWS IN AMERICA

THE first daily problem of the British exile in America to-day, and especially since the United States and Japan went to war, is to find out how the war really is going. It was never easy, even during America's period of neutrality. There was too much news then.

Now that the United States is squarely at war, from a plethora of news we have shrunk to a famine. The lid has come down with a censorship limiting war news in the main to strictly edited official communiqués. This is perhaps as it should be, but it bears hardly upon a public as avid for news, piping hot news, as the American. The morale of a country at war, and America especially, must depend very largely on a steady and reasonably informative supply of official news.

To meet this requirement during the last war the American Government set up a Committee of Public Information under the well-known publicist, George Creel, which released news to the Press upon a uniform and carefully synchronised plan resembling that of our own Ministry of Information and the B.B.C. to-day. In theory this is an ideal system, but in practice it is anathema. No journalist who ever lived sets any store on a general issue of news, for he holds that what can safely be told to everybody is of no particular value to anybody, and least of all to an American news-hawk. He wants the exclusive item which will enhance his own professional reputation and sell his paper.

George Creel's Committee was never popular, so this time the George Creel plan is scrapped and the individual journalist left to garner news as best he may. The main result is a spate of rumour and speculation and un-informed comment, both in the Press and over the radio. Much of the comment, especially in the responsibly-minded Press and radio circuits, is both intelligent and sound. But not invariably. What the public pay for is good news. Failing that, they want sensational news. Certain editors and commentators see that they get it. The very absence of official information is a help to these enterprising publicists. It leaves them free to soar into the realms of conjecture, unhampered by any of the restrictions imposed by definite knowledge.

A further result is to breed among the American people a certain complacency and false optimism which is far from being justified at this moment, and is causing serious concern to thinking Americans. The first shock of Pearl Harbour being over, the average civilian is inclined to settle back into ordinary routine, lulled to security by the President's tremendous war programme recently published, and comfortably believing now that everything is merely a matter of time. More than one public man has raised his voice of late, and passionately warned his fellow-countrymen against the evils of " smugness." But the root of this smugness is the lack of authentic news calculated to bring realisation of danger.

Moreover, the Americans incline to the personal touch and the human story. They are a nation of hero-wor-shippers. A successful young airman, immediately he is mentioned by name, is promoted by popular acclaim to the rank of ace. The first American private soldier to set foot in Northern Ireland the other day was publicised like a film star. His portrait appeared in every newspaper, and his relatives in his native Michigan were extensively interviewed.

The outstanding hero of the moment is, naturally,

General MacArthur. Nothing definite has been revealed about him save that he is beleaguered on the butt end of the peninsula of Bataan in the south of Luzon, with his back to Manila Bay. It may be found impossible to relieve or reinforce him, and the surrender or annihilation of his force may merely be a matter of time. But he is still there after two months of keeping the Stars and Stripes aloft, despite overwhelming odds, and his name has only to be mentioned in public or his face shown upon the screen to raise rapturous and well-merited cheers.

All this, of course, is healthy and stimulating to national pride and morale, but it does not help to elucidate the general situation. And it tends to obscure something else. The situation in the Philippines is very much the same as that which prevailed on the island of Singapore. In both places gallant men were fighting for their lives against heavy odds. But, in the view of the ultra-patriotic section of the American Press the one was a glorious and successful defence; the other a series of defeats and retreats. The British official communiqué was never expanded in a favourable sense. If the news was bad, that was an " admission "; if it was good, that was merely an " assertion " or a " claim." The Dutch communiqués receive much the same treatment.

This, of course, is all part and parcel of the ebullient American make-up. Wise people know no intentional disparagement of the Dutch and British effort is intended, but it is unfortunate, because it gives the average American the impression that America is not being adequately supported by her Allies. Only yesterday a young city clerk sitting behind me in the train threw down his newspaper and said to his neighbour : " Well, I guess we got to carry the whole war now." It is also baffling and discouraging to millions here who realise and admire the tremendous fight our nation is putting up.

Such little trials must be philosophically accepted as due to differences of international outlook and temperament; but there is another matter much more serious, and it should be put right at once: the suggestion—initiated by enemy propaganda and faithfully fostered by our own official communiqués—that the majority of the fighting on the British side at this moment is being done by Dominion and Indian troops, while several millions of British soldiers in Britain are doing nothing at all.

This, of course, is an old, old echo of the last war. " Britain will fight to the last Frenchman " and Australian and American. But the blame lies, and lay last time, on our own national habit and tradition of ascribing all the credit for a good job of work to the other fellow. This is called " good sportsmanship." It works out all right on the Centre Court at Wimbledon, but not in a total war.

Apart from that, we have a national passion for moderate statement—even under-statement. It never occurs to the composers of our war bulletins to lay emphasis upon what in their view ought to be taken for granted—such as the gallantry and devotion of our own native-born soldiers. Thomas Atkins, they consider, needs no pat on the back for doing his obvious duty, so they reserve their thanks and gratitude for the Dominion and other troops who have come to our aid from all over the world. But the impression created in that world is that Thomas Atkins simply is not there—or, if he is, someone else is in the forefront of the battle.

Fortunately, at long last the injustice and futility of this policy has been recognised in high quarters. This week a statement put out by the British authorities in Washington reveals that of the British Empire troops fighting in all theatres of war, between 70 and 80 per cent. were purely British. Their achievements and casualties were in proportion. That will do much good, but the impression should never have been created in the first instance, and it got a long start.

Such, then, is the situation in America to-day in regard to news—an acute shortage in some directions and considerable misconception in others. It should be added that there is a feeling among responsible people, and certainly the American Press, that the present rather oppressive secrecy is being overdone and should be modified in the interests of national morale. Effective demand for such a modification can come only from one quarter—the American nation as a whole, speaking with a single voice; but the inhabitants of this vast country are not yet collectively awake to the issues and dangers of the situation. Millions continue to follow their usual routine of leaving the successful conduct of the war to that nebulous and convenient old gentleman, Uncle Sam. Cinemas, theatres, and race-tracks are still crowded. The comforting slogan is still accepted by many as a substitute for personal exertion.

At the present moment Gilbert and Sullivan's " Mikado " is being presented at a New York theatre. In the first lines of the opening chorus, " If you want to know who we are, we are gentlemen of Japan," the producer, to avoid any appearance of favouring the country's enemies, has altered " gentlemen " to " gangsters." The audience, thoroughly reassured now that they are witnessing a first-class piece of anti-Japanese propaganda, sit back and enjoy themselves hugely—as, assuredly, must the shade of Gilbert !

All of which is reminiscent of another community not so long ago and nearer home. America will wake right up, as we have done. The sooner the better—but a judicious relaxation of the censorship would help a lot.

XXI

THE MAPLE LEAF

WEATHER reports in modern warfare are *tabu*, but it is no military secret that Canada at this time of the year is occasionally under snow. Such was the case during a visit which I paid recently to an intensely busy industrial centre not very far beyond the borders of the United States. They have plenty of snow in the United States as well, but somehow snow in Canada contrives to look whiter, more ornamental, than farther south, perhaps because there are not so many people to trample it down.

Upon the day of my arrival the sun glittered in a sky of cloudless blue, below which an unbroken mantle of snow covered the country-side. It lay upon fields and frozen water, it lay upon roofs and the branches of fir trees. It even covered the sidings of the railway yards and the grime of the coal dumps outside the factories.

But there is all the difference in the world between being under snow and being snowed under. Canada to-day is a hive of activity, whatever the weather. Canadians are more accustomed to severe winters than we are, and make their arrangements accordingly. The soldiers' barracks are centrally heated; every man wears snow-boots and headgear which provides if necessary for the protection of the ears.

This is a considerable military centre. It is the head-quarters, for instance, of a regiment of Canadian Highlanders bearing the same name as, and affiliated to, a famous Highland Regiment of Scotland in which I happen to take a loyal and sentimental interest. As with us, the kilt and the glengarry have been replaced for the duration by service dress and balmoral bonnet, but the band are still in full Highland panoply, and the triumphant skirl of their pipes is good to hear.

This town is also the home of another military establishment, and a very remarkable one—the Canadian Army Trades Schools. An army tradesman is not, as many laymen used to imagine, a camp-follower who peddles comforts to the troops ; he is a mechanical specialist—in other words, the man who keeps in running order the vast array of mechanisation upon which a modern army depends for its very life.

There are two thousand young men here, collected from all parts of Canada, undergoing what may be called an omnibus tradesman's course, under experienced sergeant instructors. They repair army lorries, incidentally educating themselves in their design and handling. They are initiated into the mysteries of wireless : here are three young men in overalls and berets who have just been handed a faulty radio receiving-set and bidden to find out what is the matter with it. They strip and assemble motor engines ; they manufacture machine tools and other instruments of precision, and practise both electric and acetylene welding. A whole corner of one workshop is occupied by figures working behind screens, sheltered by masks and goggles from the blinding flame of their apparatus.

Each of these workshops is a crowded, businesslike, and obviously happy place. These lads are all Canadian born, but not necessarily of Canadian-born parents. The majority of names, of course, are English and Scottish, but some are Italian, Russian, Polish, even German. There is a town in Ontario called Kitchener. Less than thirty years ago it was called Berlin, and when upon the outbreak of the last war the name was changed to one with more patriotic appeal, there was a pretty outcry from its Germanic inhabitants. But there would be no trouble to-day ; this generation has done with Berlin and all its works, long ago.

There are large numbers, naturally, of French Canadians. Practically none of these can speak English, but they have asked not to be segregated in one barrack, but to be dispersed among the English-speaking huts, to give them an opportunity to learn the language. This is a most healthy sign, and incidentally a very significant step to anyone who knows the mentality of the Habitant of Quebec.

The barrack huts themselves are one-storied wooden buildings of standard pattern, and it is pleasant to see the old London street names, which used to be a familiar feature of our camps and communication trenches in the last war, such as " Piccadilly," painted up at the corner of a block. The men take their meals in a regular mess-hall with kitchen adjoining, and not where they have slept, which means that food does not have to be carried through the open air from a distant cookhouse. It is served by mess orderlies, English fashion. Herein the practice differs from that of the United States Army, which employs the cafeteria system. An American mess hut, working at full pressure, can pass a thousand diners through in an hour. This, of course, is characteristic of our two countries. An American feels that unless he does everything at top speed he is wasting time ; the Britisher, either from natural indolence or out of respect for his stomach, likes to take his time over his victuals.

Another divergence from American usage is that whereas American soldiers sleep upon low iron bedsteads, the Canadians employ double-deckers, reminiscent of those which have become such a familiar adjunct of our own Tube stations in London.

The town itself supports innumerable industries, based mainly upon steel, and work is maintained all round the clock. The only difference is that whereas those great plants used to produce agricultural machinery, electric appliances and the like, they are now turning out guns, machine guns, and shells. Most of them were converted from peace to war service after the French collapse of 1940, and have been going all out this long while. At almost any hour of the day you may hear a distant boom, followed by a soft plop-plop in the sky above your head, reviving familiar and not altogether reassuring memories ; and if you look up, you will see little balls of cotton-wool, as it were, disintegrating and drifting away in the blue. These come from a new A.A. battery being tested on the range a few miles away.

But the chief preoccupation of this busy district, and, indeed, of the whole of the Dominion of Canada to-day and for a given period, is the raising of money. Wars have to be paid for, and the drive for the Victory Loan of 1942 is on. Our particular township has pledged itself to raise twenty million dollars, and will do so.

An elaborate and ingenious publicity campaign is in progress, with the whole business strength of the town behind it, and no one has any excuse for not knowing exactly how much money is required, what it is required for, and what his own contribution should be. Put simply, Canada expects during 1942 to spend the sum of three thousand five hundred million dollars, or to put it the American way, three and a half billions, or, roughly, seven hundred million pounds sterling. Of this sum, one-half is to be raised by taxation from all sources, the other by a loan, or, as the official appeal tersely and properly puts it, " by borrowing from your savings." On a basis of population this means that every man, woman and child in Canada must contribute something over three hundred dollars per head, half in taxation, half in loan. This quota, it is emphasised, is well within the means of people who are nearly all earning good money in war production.

The loan is made up by buying Defence Stamps for small amounts, or Victory Bonds up to any denomination —very much the same system, in fact, as that of our War Savings Certificates. When you have accumulated enough stamps you can exchange them for a Bond. In many shops and places of entertainment patrons are asked to take their change in stamps, and almost invariably do. It is further pointed out that workers to-day, by expending part of their considerable wages in Bonds, are not only helping to win the war, but are making an excellent investment against probable lean times when the war is over. It should be added that in Canada to-day not far short of two million people are engaged in war production, apart from over four hundred thousand serving in the Forces.

The United States, incidentally, employs almost similar methods of financing the war. Income tax has been stepped up to towering heights, and has been extended to millions of people who have never paid income tax before. To stimulate the patriotic enthusiasms of these, and to educate them in the proper manner of filling up income tax forms, the Government have enlisted the services of a most unexpected preceptor, our old friend Donald Duck, no less. He appears upon the screen attended by his three disreputable nephews, in their usual cricket caps. After listening to a brief broadcast upon the whole duty of the taxpayer, Donald becomes fired with raucous enthusiasm, and announces his intention of paying his income tax forthwith. He is supplied with a form, and with the aid of an animated and talkative fountain pen, puts himself down as an actor, unmarried—I had never realised before that he was a bachelor—with three dependents. His income he computes at two thousand five hundred dollars. This sounds a modest emolument for such a screen headliner, but the purpose of the film is to explain to the man of small means in the audience exactly how to fill up a tax form and what remissions he may demand. We see a close-up of the form, with the net amount due in taxation ; and the picture closes with Donald's cheque whizzing across the United States from Hollywood to Washington. The whole thing is admirably done, and, despite the criticisms of certain Congressional purists, makes excellent propaganda.

But that by the way. Let us revert to a final aspect of the Canadian War Loan. The most arresting feature of the appeal is not the description of how the money is to be raised, but the statement as to how it is to be spent. The statement is quite brief. It says :

1. For our own war costs, 2,000 millions.
2. To aid Britain, 1,000 millions.
3. For the cost of Government, 500 millions.

If you ask what sort of aid to Britain is indicated under item two the answer may surprise you. It certainly surprised me. You will be informed in the most matter-of-fact fashion that the figure represents a remission by the Canadian people of a thousand million dollars of the sum due from the people of Britain for war supplies from Canada. Our total indebtedness to Canada under this head for the current year will be in the neighbourhood of 1,500 million dollars ; and Canada, of her own volition and as a gesture of goodwill and affection, has forgiven us two-thirds of our obligation. Just that. A nation of eleven million people, burdened with a colossal war bill of its own, will put paid in full to a little matter of a thousand million, just to help the Old Country. Do we know about this at home ? Is it realised ? If not, let people be told, and told far and near.

Such is Canada—young, vigorous, resolute, generous—a strong wind from the west, well calculated to disperse some of the mists of doubt and difficulty which to-day hang over the Eastern horizon.

XXII

SEARCH FOR SCAPEGOATS

BAD news in war-time is a searching test of national morale. The United States has now been at war for ten weeks. What is the national attitude to-day?

The sudden and humiliating visitation of Pearl Harbour did two things—it ended once and for all the doctrine of " all aid to the Allies short of war," and it united the country solidly behind the President for the first time. As already related, America went fighting mad overnight; an enormous programme of wartime production was launched and acclaimed. Then everybody sat down and waited for quick results and hot news. Uncle Sam's hat was in the ring; the rest was a foregone conclusion.

But the results, though some of them were quick enough, were the reverse of what had been expected, and the hotter the news the colder the comfort. The Pacific Ocean, the particular preserve and charge of the American Navy, has passed for the time being into Japanese hands. Only in one corner of the island of Luzon in the Philippines do American troops still hold out, and, despite their courage and the high qualities of General MacArthur, their fate seems merely to be a matter of time. On the eastern seaboard, again, up and down the Atlantic coast, and almost within sight of land, twenty-one ships, totalling a tonnage of over a hundred thousand, have been sunk by German submarines within the past few weeks. The whereabouts and activities of the American Navy itself, except for a brisk raid upon some Japanese shipping near the Marshall Islands, are a profound secret—and the American people do not like secrets.

To crown the general and growing spirit of disappointment and dissatisfaction, the huge and stately *Normandie*, undergoing transformation into an army transport under the direction of the Admiral commanding the Third Naval District, has been completely gutted by fire, and now lies on her side for all to see, " like a dead elephant," at her berth in New York Harbour—a truly piteous spectacle, especially for one who has enjoyed her speed and comfort in happier days. It is more than doubtful if she can ever be raised to an even keel again. The origin of the fire is a complete mystery ; but that so enormous a vessel could have been so completely enveloped in flames in so short a time points either to unbelievable carelessness or most efficient sabotage.

The smoke of the burning *Normandie*, drifting across New York itself, got right home. For the moment the misfortunes of the Atlantic and Pacific fronts were forgotten in a burst of public indignation over something which need never have happened. A New York evening paper, *PM*, published a series of articles revealing that a short time before the disaster actually took place, a reporter from that paper, in order to test the value of any precautions which the Third Naval District might be taking against sabotage in American transports and other vitally important shipping, dressed himself up as a labourer, joined the Longshoreman's Union, paying twenty-six dollars for the privilege, and spent two or three days on board the *Normandie*. No one seems to have attempted to supervise him or give him any work to do. He simply roamed about at will, taking notes of vulnerable spots wherein to plant a bomb or start a conflagration, if he or anyone else so desired. When he had seen enough he wrote his report and handed it to his editor, who forwarded it to the responsible naval authority, stating that the information which it contained would not be published, but suggesting that immediate action should be taken in the matter. The only reply was to the effect that if the reporter trespassed upon the *Normandie* again he risked being shot.

This unhappy chain of disaster has led to the inevitable result. A spirited and impatient people find themselves brought up short in what was confidently expected to be a march of efficient and victorious progress. So a search for scapegoats begins. The British public are familiar enough with these witch hunts ; we have been holding one in our own island quite recently. The target in our own case is usually the Government, or a member thereof. There is a natural reluctance to criticise the fighting forces themselves, who, whatever their measure of success or failure, are usually doing their job at the risk of their lives. So we direct our heavy artillery upon the statesmen and politicians who in our view have failed to devote sufficient vision and energy to the conduct of the war.

American public censure follows much the same course, except that it usually refrains from direct criticism of the President, who, besides being the leader of a party, represents in himself the sovereignty of the American people as a whole, and as such is above partisan attack. But Congress is not immune, and Congress, to put the matter vulgarly, is at the present moment getting it in the neck. It should be added that Congress has been extending its neck this long while.

People are being reminded that some years ago, when the Administration proposed to fortify the island of Guam, the most important link in the chain of ocean stations which connect the Philippines and the China coast with Hawaii and California, the scheme was voted down by Congress as being too expensive and too provocative; and that more recently, less than a year ago in fact, when America stood upon the very brink of war, Congress was so completely insensible to stark facts and patriotic duty that a Bill designed to keep America's newly-drafted army in commission for a further period, and prevent its personnel from being dispersed to their homes, was only carried by a single vote. There are further accusations, some of them true, that money appropriations for the construction of munition plants and ship-building yards have been deliberately obstructed by individuals or groups in Congress, with a view to having the *locale* of these lucrative utilities shifted to their own constituencies.

Still, these political delinquencies might have been forgiven, or at least overlooked, had not members of Congress selected one of the most critical periods in American history, a few weeks ago, to embark upon a scheme for providing themselves with pensions. This was a little too much. Congress found itself compared to the fiddling Emperor Nero, greatly to the latter's advantage; a band of humorists in the Middle West started a charitable society to provide " Bundles for Congress "; and Congress, most of whose members are due to come up for re-election in the course of this year, hastily bowed to the storm. As I write, the Senate has quashed its own pension vote by a majority of seventy-five to five, and the House of Representatives is in process of following suit.

Needless to say, scapegoat hunting has not been confined to members of Congress. The O.C.D., or Organisation for Civil Defence, of which Mrs. Roosevelt has been a prominent member, has been getting into trouble for engaging an allegedly communistic film actor to supervise entertainment for the troops, and an alleged " fan dancer " to organise physical training for the young women of America. This insignificant hullabaloo is of no importance whatsoever except that it furnishes a direct avenue of attack upon the White House itself, via Mrs. Roosevelt—an avenue of which the President's personal opponents have been availing themselves for some time. But Mrs. Roosevelt has now very sensibly resigned from the O.C.D., and the avenue has been closed to political traffic.

Neither is the hunt confined to the United States. Needless to say, that hapless island, Great Britain, is getting its full share of attention. Singapore, the Burma Road, the *Gneisenau* and the *Scharnhorst*, even Mr. Churchill himself, have come under a storm of comment and criticism —some of it just and true, most of it ill informed, and all of it untimely and discouraging.

For some reason the escape of the two battle-cruisers from Brest has caused more stir and censure than the loss of Singapore. This is in a way a compliment, for whatever opinion Americans may hold of the British Army, they have a sincere belief, and rightly, in the might of the British Navy. But they can never quite visualise or focus our naval commitments in detail, especially in home waters. The fact that Germany now holds every yard of the western coast of Europe, and are as strong along the French coast as we are along the English, and that it was, therefore, no harder for the enemy to protect the escaping ships from the air than it was for us to attack them— much easier, in fact—never seems to have come home to critics who have habitually regarded the English Channel as a kind of private back alley which any Englishman ought to be able to block.

As for our misfortunes by land, it was inevitable that the circumstances that Singapore had been lost by the British, while the Americans were still contriving to maintain a foothold in the Philippines, should be played up to

I

the limit. Human nature being what it is, that comparison, though not on all fours, is understandable and pardonable. But criticism of our army in other quarters has outrun reasonable limits, and is indeed assuming dangerous proportions, for nothing is so disturbing to the confidence of a country at war as an implanted doubt as to the reliability of its allies. Here, undoubtedly, the Fifth Column has been hard at work. The British forces are consistently belittled as ill-trained and incompetently led. There are the usual dreary catchwords—brass hats, monocles, spit-and-polish, all in the best vein of our own stay-at-home strategists. Irresponsible columnists have begun to contribute to the lower-grade press a stream of cheap disparagement of an army which for nearly two and a half years, at one time entirely single-handed, has been shedding its blood all over the world to preserve human freedom in the New World as well as in the Old. So unworthy have been some of the allegations regarding the efficiency and even courage of our men, that the *New York Times*, the leading newspaper of the United States, has just published, in a very timely article from its military correspondent, a most just and generous tribute to our army and its achievements. This article has been acclaimed by every friend of ours in America, and their name is legion.

But all these, of course, are the natural reactions of a great civil community which, after generations of sheltered prosperity, suddenly finds itself confronted with the perplexities of total war upon its own doorstep, front and back. We have been through the same experience ourselves in an even more acute degree, and though we cannot entirely agree with the misgivings of the American people regarding our efficiency, we can at least sympathise with them in the problems and perils so familiar to ourselves, with which they find themselves faced to-day.

America inevitably has a long way to go before she can

realise the full extent of her responsibilities, and adjust herself to the Allied scheme. Her population is vast, and much education will be necessary, as all wise and patriotic Americans recognise, often with genuine concern. To millions of their fellow-countrymen this is still just another war. Only last week the Brooklyn Dodgers, New York's pet baseball team, departed in two specially chartered aircraft to Havana, " to commence their spring training in a suitable climate "—all except two members, who could not come to a satisfactory arrangement with their employers as to the number of thousands of dollars per annum essential to the remuneration of their labours. An American enlisted soldier gets thirty dollars a month. But the show must go on ; the Dodgers must dodge.

To-night the President is to give a broadcast talk to his countrymen. He has promised to be frank. Perhaps he will be audible in Havana.

XXIII

A CLOSE-UP OF THE PRESIDENT

As already noted, what we are all crying out for in these days, on either side of the Atlantic, is reliable information, stable intelligence—something straight from the horse's mouth. At home in England we get it from our own Prime Minister's periodical reports to the House of Commons. Those pronouncements, with their blunt candour, their grim humour, and their unquenchable courage, are the prop and mainstay of our faith as a nation and as an Empire to-day.

In Washington Congress possesses no Prime Minister, no Front Bench, no single representative source of information at all. Two nights ago, Los Angeles and Hollywood had their first air-raid alarm, and celebrated that *première* with characteristic enthusiasm. Guns roared, searchlights swept the skies, and anti-aircraft shells burst over many miles of the Californian coast, from the small hours until daylight. No aircraft were hit, and no bombs were dropped. The only casualties were buildings damaged and individuals injured by falling shell-splinters. Naturally everyone was enquiring next morning how many enemy bombers had been employed in the operation, and as no immediate information was forthcoming, the Press felt itself at liberty to publish its own estimates, varying with the politics of the paper and the editorial imagination.

Later in the day, however, two official statements were issued, one by the Secretary for War to the effect that the raiders numbered fifteen or twenty, were of civilian make, came from hidden American bases, and were operated by Fifth Columnists. The second came from the Secretary of the Navy, who tersely dismissed the entire episode as " a false alarm."

This sort of thing naturally confuses the public mind and therefore whenever America wants what it calls " the real dope " it turns, very sensibly, to the fountain-head, to the President himself. And this makes the President's bi-weekly meeting with the Press, every Tuesday and Friday, an event of outstanding importance to a hundred million news-hungry people.

Admittance to these conferences is a close-guarded privilege, and every correspondent has firstly to establish his own *bona fides* and secondly convince the authorities that the paper or papers which he represents are sufficiently important to be included. There are some eighty or ninety of these regular correspondents. They are mostly known by name and sight to the White House officials, and form a close corporation. Indeed, it is difficult for a casual observer to gain admittance at all. Last week, however, to my great gratification, and thanks to the " pull " of a friend at court, I found myself attending one of these mysteries, and incidentally enjoying my first encounter with the President in the flesh. I stood within four feet of him for half an hour.

Let me begin by describing the scene. These conferences are held at the White House, the President's official residence, in what is called the Oval Room. It is not a big room; it is perhaps thirty feet long, beautifully proportioned and classic in design, with lightly coloured walls adorned by pictures, mostly water-colours or aquatints of ships of the early steamboat period—about the time, in fact, that the White House was built, or rather rebuilt. Across one end of the room is a wooden screen covered with maps.

The other end of the oval forms a natural bow-window, and here the President is seated at a low desk, with his back to the light. Behind his chair, upon polished vertical staves, droop the Stars and Stripes and the Presidential flag. Through the windows you can see the sunny White House gardens, with here and there an armed policeman or patrol. The White House domain to-day is very closely guarded indeed—far more closely, on the surface, at any rate, than Downing Street.

A year or two ago Press conferences and I were no strangers to one another. Indeed, it was part of my duty to summon one of these, at regular intervals, to a White-hall council-chamber, where the assembled Press correspondents might be addressed by, or could administer the third degree to, some eminent and reluctant military expert. This memory made the differences of procedure in the Oval Room profoundly interesting. The most marked of these is due to the fact that the President, owing to the physical infirmity from which he has suffered ever since his younger days, and which he appears to the outward eye to carry so lightly, is unable to move about without assistance. (How many of us have ever seen a portrait or film of Franklin Roosevelt otherwise than seated or standing supported? That very reflection gives us some measure of the indomitable fortitude of the man.) But the result is that whereas most public speakers are accustomed to present themselves to an assembled and waiting audience, and address them standing while the audience sit, in the White House it is the audience which presents itself to the speaker and stands while he remains seated. This circumstance exercises a curious psychological influence upon the atmosphere of the conference. It gives us a kind of feeling, especially in these temple-like surroundings, that we are not so much taking part in a press conference as consulting the Oracle.

Not that there is any sort of mystery about Sir Oracle himself. His very desk is enough to dispel the suggestion of formality. It is adorned with a multiplicity of small and unexpected articles, such as china dogs, brass gadgets, wooden toys and other mascots. The President has a well-known weakness for collecting such souvenirs, and is reputed never to abandon one once he has acquired it. Incidentally, it is not by any means easy to get a glimpse of these interesting exhibits, or even to see the President himself; indeed, for quite three-quarters of the assembled company it is impossible, for the room is crowded and the front rank stands pressed right up against the desk. The President could shake hands with half a dozen of them without leaning forward. There are further ranks in the rear, close packed. Only a few determined thrusters or those endowed with unusual inches can get a direct view at all. That was why, it may be remembered, in this very room not so long ago, Mr. Churchill obligingly stood upon a chair in order to give all present a satisfactory eyeful.

Now for the President himself. He is wearing a light grey suit, with a black band round his left arm, presumably in memory of his late mother. He is much younger-looking, and has a much healthier colour than one would imagine from the visions of him presented to us by that most unflattering medium, the close-up film. No heavy lines are discernible in his face, and the black shadows under his eyes, so noticeable on the screen, are no longer there. He has a noble head, with shrewd, humorous eyes, and a fine pair of shoulders.

He has certain mannerisms. He smokes perpetual cigarettes, in a holder even longer than that once sported by Edgar Wallace. So much is it a part of him on these occasions that some people call it his sceptre. His general air is that of a slightly tired man, which for that matter most of us are at present. When he ponders a reply he passes his disengaged hand slowly over his brow. When listening to a question he leans back comfortably and puffs out his cheeks. When he scores a point he purses his mouth into a little round " o," and glances up quizzically at his victim. But the main impression that he gives, as he confronts that sea of faces, is that of a man perfectly at ease and entire master of the situation.

His audience, by the way, is composed almost entirely of men. Many of these are famous themselves—the star correspondents of some of the most important newspapers in the world—the civilised world, that is. There are only four or five women. One of them is an unexpected young person of the glamour girl type, with no hat and some snowdrops in her coiffure. One cannot help wondering what particular organ she represents. The others are normal enough, and ask some shrewd and useful questions.

So much for the setting, the company, and the central

figure. Now for the general procedure. At home in England we follow a set routine. The speaker for the day is briefly introduced, or introduces himself, tells his tale, and then invites questions, which he deals with, sometimes in considerable detail, one by one. But here the proceedings are less formal, more fluid. The conference practically takes the form of a running fire of questions, answers, interjections, and wisecracks, and the President seems to enjoy every moment of it. It is not easy to realise that every word he utters is being chosen with the utmost care, for at any moment some lightly-spoken impromptu may be taken for gospel and published as such. Occasionally he prefaces a remark with : " Remember, this is off the record ! " meaning that this particular item is for private information and not for publication ; and it is the journalist's first law never to abuse that confidence. That is why some of his most interesting observations at this particular conference cannot be quoted here.

Occasionally, however, he comes out with a very direct statement indeed—and he means it to be direct.

" Is it true, Mr. President, that the Secretary for —— is about to resign ? "

" It is not true. It is a flat lie put out to embarrass the Administration. I shall be glad if you will contradict it."

Sometimes, too, the President utilises the occasion to introduce to public notice some fresh legislation contemplated by the Executive. Upon this occasion he read to the company a summary of a new and important Housing Bill, shortly to be submitted to Congress. This is another contrast with British procedure and strange to our ideas, for with us Parliament must be the first to hear of such matters. But the President of the United States is not responsible to Congress for his actions, and can employ the Press to publicise a scheme which, in our case, would have to be submitted in the first instance, by the responsible Minister, to the House of Commons.

But in the main and on the whole during these conferences the President gives the impression of a man fencing—tactfully, warily, humorously, and with consummate skill.

" What happened to that Japanese submarine that shelled the oil-refinery near Santa Barbara yesterday, Mr. President ? Has it been taken care of ? "

Here is a leading question—a definite attempt to probe a naval secret. The President looks up quizzically.

" My information," he replies, " is that the submarine is now under water."

" Voluntarily ? "

" Ah ! " And that is all that the questioner gets. But another takes his place.

" In your broadcast last night, Mr. President, you lashed out at the rumour-mongers. Just whom had you in mind ? "

" Just exactly the same individuals that you have in yours ! "

There is a big laugh at that, and the meeting breaks up. It has not been an unusual or exciting session ; nothing of special importance or interest has cropped up. But everybody has had a chance to ask his questions, and everybody has been answered. Whether the answer has conveyed any positive information is another matter. Still, the occasion has served its purpose—the maintenance of a general sense of personal contact and nearness to the source.

Meanwhile I reflect, as I run the gauntlet of the police guard at the gate, that I should have liked to be present at the next Conference, if only because then the President will certainly be asked to reconcile the statements of the Secretary for War and the Secretary of the Navy concerning the Los Angeles episode. I have no doubt he will be equal to the occasion.

XXIV

BRITISH WINGS OVER AMERICA

ONE of the first things that the visitor to the United States has to get used to in these days is to take air-travel as a matter of course.

Train services are numerous, and more efficient than ever. But this land of vast distances is inhabited by a people whose main object in life appears to be to get from one point to another as swiftly as possible, whether it be from New York to Chicago or from the ground floor to the fiftieth ; and therefore no one dreams of spending, say, two nights and a day in a train when he can accomplish the same journey by air between breakfast and dinner—or rather, if he can afford to do so, for air-travel is expensive.

Of American railway travel I have already written that its outstanding feature is its complete standardisation of service, especially in the matter of through connexions, sleeping accommodation, and catering arrangements. But the Air Services have established a standard too. It might be described as a standard of immaculate slickness. Being unable to compete with the railways in the matter of low fares, they employ all the resources of super-salesmanship to attract custom in other ways. Their ticket-offices are palatial, and service-with-a-smile is the order of the day.

Instead of queueing up at a pigeon-hole with a morose and monosyllabic ticket-clerk behind it, the customer confides his wants to a dapper young man in chromium surroundings, who looks up schedules for him, reassures him about weather prospects, informs him that a " complimentary lunch " will be served to him on board the plane, and pronounces a sort of benediction over him as he hands him his change.

The plane itself is a silvery giant carrying about twenty passengers in small arm-chairs, double on one side of the aisle, single on the other. Your smallest wants are attended to by a slim young man in maroon trousers and a buff-coloured Eton jacket, or by a glamorous " hostess " dressed in a uniform somewhat resembling that of our own Women's Royal Air Force. These seem to be able to preserve perfect balance in their numerous passages up and down the aisles, here to help a passenger to adjust his safety-belt, there to hand you a map of the route, or warn you politely against smoking until the plane leaves the ground. They also distribute chewing-gum, the mastication of which is supposed to relieve the pressure upon the ear-drums caused by changes in atmospheric pressure. Some of us, however, prefer a pain in the ear-drums.

As for the " complimentary " meals, to find yourself eight thousand feet up in the air, with a neat celluloid tray upon your knees furnished with chicken casserole, hot coffee, ice-cream and cake, is a small miracle in itself, the most surprising part of the miracle being that you take the meal and its preparation as the merest matter of course. But to sail above the clouds at two hundred miles an hour under a blazing sun, while frost and snow hold the earth bound beneath you, is a little upsetting to one's sense of proportion in any case.

Incidentally these ministering angels are not allowed to

accept tips—a circumstance which relieves the passenger from all the coat-brushing, shoe-wiping, and other superfluous attentions so invariable in the case of our old friend Pullman George, conscientiously and remorselessly earning his twenty-five cents.

Night travel by air offers fewer attractions. A sleeper-plane reproduces, in tabloid form, too much of the discomfort and publicity of the ordinary Pullman. There is no room for luggage, so you improvise your toilet as best you may. Your upper or lower berth is about as large as a coffin, and you are acutely conscious both of the proximity and nocturnal wrigglings of the gentleman or lady immediately above or below you. Upon one of my recent journeys there was a baby too. It is difficult to sleep the night through, because the plane makes periodical descents to the ground, and the change in atmospheric pressure already mentioned usually sets your ears throbbing and awakens you. Still, you can cover two thousand miles overnight, and your strenuous American will accept almost any discomfort at that price.

A few days ago I took an air journey under different auspices and in a very different conveyance—a two-seater American Army plane, travelling over Florida. I was on my way to visit one of the British Flying Training Schools which have been established in the United States. My position was cramped; on the other hand my range of vision was unlimited, which is not the case when one is boxed up in a passenger plane.

Florida is famed for its warmth, sunshine, and tropical luxuriance. It is a State in which you may see cocoanuts growing upon palm-trees, and pick oranges and grapefruit by the road-side. But from above Florida does not look so attractive. The greater part of it is flat, sterile, and sandy. The soil, as in California, responds readily to irrigational treatment, but water is not always available.

From my cockpit, at such times as I was not studying the fascinating array of gadgets on the instrument-board—the duplicates of those being operated by the pilot in the front seat—and wrestling with a childish longing to push a button or pull a switch, just to see what would happen, I could survey an endless expanse of brownish herbage, whitish sand and shallow stagnant pools of water, some of them broadening out into small lakes. Directly below us I could just discern a thin line of roadway, running dead straight to the horizon. Not a cheerful landscape.

But everything is useful for something, especially in war-time, and the soil and climate of Florida, not to mention Florida's wide-open spaces, are well adapted for the construction of aerodromes and instruction in the art of flying.

We were on our way to visit such an aerodrome now. Indeed, we were almost over it, though the fact was not apparent. An aerodrome is usually recognisable from almost any height, because the concrete runways, radiating in different directions and intersecting at the centre, form a standard pattern something like a Union Jack. But no such distinguishing marks were apparent as we began to circle down—only some hangars, barrack huts, grounded planes, and a windsock blowing out horizontally, for the weather was squally.

This particular airfield, though it will ultimately be one of the largest in the world, is brand new to-day, and although it is already in use, the runways have not yet been concreted. Still, we took the ground with hardly a bump, and in a few moments we had taxied over the uneven turf and come to a standstill before the School Headquarters.

Here my American pilot, whose official position in the School was that of a Flying Instructor, handed me over to my compatriots, having first expressed his readiness to fly me back, in my own good time, whence I came.

It was pleasant to see the Royal Air Force uniform again, and hear English voices and talk solid British shop. We were able to exchange quite a lot of information, for I had heard little reliable news of our own air operations for some time, while my hosts, marooned in the heart of a wilderness of sand and water, were hungry for such crumbs of home and social intelligence as I could provide. " American radio news," they said, " is plentiful enough and varied enough for anybody, goodness knows ; but it's so pepped up and repetitious, besides being all interspersed with advertisement for patent medicines and breakfast foods, that it's hard to give it a right value. What wouldn't we give for an English Sunday newspaper, delivered regularly ! "

However, there were no complaints or repinings over the life they were living or the work they were doing. The School is a school in every sense of the word—an American school run by American teachers for British pupils, to whom they provide tuition and board, as at any public or preparatory school at home, except that the bills at the end of term are paid by the British Government. The supervision, discipline and welfare of the cadets are in the hands of an experienced group of R.A.F. officers ; otherwise the establishment is entirely American-run. There are several such schools in the United States to-day, situated in States where the climate and weather conditions are suitable for flying instruction all the year round—in Florida, Texas, California, Oklahoma, and Arizona. In addition, British pupils are attending various purely American Flying Schools, for special instruction in some particular duty, such as navigation or wireless operating. What tales these temporary exiles will have to tell when they get home, and what an invaluable education, not merely for them but for their instructors and hosts !

But in this camp they are merely being exercised, so to speak, in the grammar and syntax of airmanship. There are about two hundred of them—boys from all parts of Britain and all walks of life. In normal times they would be beginning to consider the choice of some stereotyped trade or profession. But to-day that choice has been made for them. They have been plucked by blind necessity from their homes, their class-rooms, their cricket-nets, and whirled over some thousands of miles of ocean to a land which has only heard of baseball, to be initiated into the most individual and adventurous of all Services. Beyond a few hours spent in the air at home, to ascertain if the pupil is sufficiently air-minded to repay further instruction, they arrive here complete novices—novices, too, in what may be called the American way of life.

Here, needless to say, their path has been made easy in many directions. Offers of hospitality pour in upon them. They are invited to visit Florida homes as far away as Palm Beach or Miami, and to spend week-ends, prolonged week-ends, with all and sundry. Indeed their commander, the senior R.A.F. officer, confesses that he has incurred a certain unpopularity among would-be hosts and hostesses for occasionally refusing leave on the ground that his charges have come to Florida to work.

Still, recreational facilities are plentiful enough, and refreshingly British. Just off the aerodrome you may see grounds marked out for football, where both Rugger and Soccer goalposts rear their heads in lofty rivalry. There is an excellent swimming-pool, and a big recreation hut for the long evenings, where various indoor games can be played. It is also furnished with an elaborate radio set, which is chronically out of action, one hears, owing to the attentions of various amateur experts. There is even a cinema, with a fresh picture twice a week. Barrack accommodation is roomy and comfortable, and there is a real dining-hall on the English plan, where you may sit at table upon a chair with a back to it, and eat a meal served by mess orderlies, instead of queueing up at a counter for it.

The course is thorough ; it lasts for more than six months. At the end of that time the instructors have convoyed their charges to the stage at which they are ready for operational training—and in these days that training is chiefly imparted by the enemy. Hereafter our young argonauts are liable to be sent almost anywhere— home again for a spell, or to India, or Libya, or the Far East. So they spread their wings and fly off into the unknown, aware only that wherever they go they will be badly wanted and that they have a tremendous tradition to live up to.

They will bear away with them lasting memories of a great and kindly country, and leave behind them, it is hoped, an equally happy impression.

XXV

DESIRE AND PERFORMANCE

" SEND me one hundred skilled mechanics under forty years of age—and send them yesterday ! "

This singular pronouncement is quoted in order to illustrate the latest American phrase for prompt, intensive action. Response to an order must be so swift, in other words, that the goods are delivered before they were asked for. And this will serve as a convenient text for my present theme.

I wrote not long ago about the difficulty experienced by Americans in finding out how the war is really going. A second and even greater difficulty is to obtain accurate information regarding the amount of war material actually being put out in America to-day.

The root of the trouble lies in the circumstance that in American business circles successful salesmanship takes precedence over everything else.

If you can talk someone into buying a pig in a poke, or for that matter overcome his " sales resistance " to the extent of selling him something he does not need, you are a Grade A business man. Not long ago, to while away a railway journey—incidentally, I have travelled some twenty thousand miles since I reached this country last September—I purchased at a news-stand in a Mid-Western station a book with the arresting title, " Sizzle-manship." It told you how to increase the sale of your goods—tooth paste, breakfast food, corn cures, ladies' underclothing—by exercising a novel, high-powered, and unexpected line of what is known as sales talk. That was Sizzlemanship. If you were content to dispose of your wares by more modest devices, that was only Fizzleman-ship.

In our own country I think we are a little inclined to be suspicious of such methods, for we are a canny race, and feel somehow that if goods have to be pushed too hard, there must be something wrong with them. But in America people seem perfectly ready, even eager, to acquiesce in a manufacturer's enthusiastic appreciation of his own shop window. " The public *likes* to be fooled," said Barnum long ago, and Barnum was right.

Unfortunately Sizzlemanship does not guarantee any special merit in the goods supplied, or, indeed, that the goods will invariably be delivered. And here is where Sizzlemanship in war-time is a positive menace, especially to an eager, sanguine, and intensely credulous people. To-day the average American is in danger of accepting soothing syrup and wishful thinking as his regular ration. He accepts tales of great ships launched daily, of tanks turned out in hundreds, and aircraft in thousands, as a mere matter of course and natural evidence of America's greatness. Further into that matter he is not interested to inquire.

Thoughtful Americans—and their numbers are increasing —are deeply and rightly concerned about this. They remember the surplus of promise and the deficit of performance in the last war, and they are anxious to know whether production to-day is keeping abreast of schedule, and, if not, how far it is dropping behind. Visible portents are not reassuring. Strikes are reported with monotonous regularity; there is more than a suggestion of sabotage about many an industrial or mechanical breakdown. They know that output is being retarded by battles over such matters of the forty-hour week and the demand of various Unions for double pay for Sundays or overtime. They know, on the authority of the Russian Ambassador, that whereas Britain's quota of equipment promised to Russia has been delivered in full, America's quota has fallen seriously short. Unfortunately these facts do not penetrate to the average American, whose reading is usually confined to the more optimistic headlines. He has a comfortable feeling, too, that things must come right in the end for a country of such vast resources and limitless enterprise as the United States. But this is a war in which the only thing that really counts is speed.

That is the disturbing side of the picture. On the other hand, we know that countless industrial plants throughout America are working smoothly and efficiently, many of them on a seven-day and twenty-four-hour basis. More than three months ago, in Cincinnati, I visited a factory which had previously manufactured carburettors, and was now turning out seventeen thousand fuses a day for a certain type of British shell. Indeed, almost anywhere the traveller goes to-day in America he may behold huge plants in full operation, and more going up.

And this daily tale of new ships is not mere publicity. Last week I was shown by a friend of mine, highly placed in the shipping industry, a series of three photographs, taken from the air. The first depicted a river estuary, with bare, flat, marshy ground on either side. At one point upon the left bank a muddy creek ran inward. The second photograph showed the land drained, the creek enlarged, and buildings going up. In the third the buildings were completed, a line of railroad had been laid down, and the creek had been converted into a spacious shipyard, with many ships building.

" That first photograph," my friend said, " was taken thirteen months ago ; the second just six months later. The third shows the general lay-out to-day. The first ship's keel was laid at the end of last September, and the ship itself will be launched in a week's time. Thereafter we expect to launch ships regularly, at the rate of two a week. We can certainly do things if we like ! " They certainly can.

Here, then, was a small but heartening sidelight upon one aspect of the situation, and I felt encouraged to go further ; so I betook myself to an official of high experience in a vast automobile concern in Detroit, the third city in America and America's principal arsenal to-day.

The official himself was a typically American product, of the type which only America can produce. He was not American born ; he had arrived from his native Netherlands unable to speak English. He had taken shrewd advantage of the educational benefits which America showers upon her adopted sons, and now, in his middle age, had worked his way up from the apprentice's bench to a commanding position in a combine which controlled four famous American motor companies, all in Detroit. Upon his upward path he had contrived to acquire the prestige and authority of a captain of industry without shedding any of his technical expertness or homespun philosophy of life.

"Sure, I know," he said. "Folks are blaming us because we are so slow. They say if we used to be turning out two thousand five hundred automobiles in a day, can't we turn out maybe two hundred and fifty tanks in the same time ? I say yes, right now, but that would only be shoemaking." By "shoemaking" he meant turning out tanks individually, by hand. "There's only one way to carry out the Presidential programme, and that's by mass production. And you can't start mass production overnight."

Then he told me some things about mass production which revealed what a very long start you give your enemy when you engage in a world war without war-production plant or machine tools.

"Mass production," he said, "is one of those things that has to be thought out and thought out—almost a philosophy, in fact. You must make sure of four things. The first is absolute accuracy of manufacture, so that you can scramble maybe six cars in a heap on the floor and construct six equally good cars out of the mixed parts. Secondly, there must be an ordered flow along the endless belt of the production line—chassis, wheels, engine, fenders, body, all swinging into place when their turn comes. Like a pig travelling down the line in a Chicago packing house, except that in Chicago they're not assembling the pig. Thirdly, you must save time and labour by a minimum of steps and movements. Lastly, there must be a remorseless inspection. We must never disappoint the customer, or we're sunk.

" In this particular plant," he continued, " we are turning out thirty-one ton tanks in place of automobiles. Think what that means in the way of conversion. We have to rebuild the whole place, to begin with. But what really takes time is *designing*, because the final design must be incapable of improvement. Do you know how long it took to design the model of your 1942 car ? "

I replied that I had not been able to afford a car since 1936, and that the car in question had been bombed in London last winter, anyway.

" Well, it takes a year," he said. " We make small clay models of every part, then full-size wooden working models, then blue prints, hundreds of them, to be checked and rechecked. In one of our tanks there are forty-five thousand rivets ; in one of our automobiles there were only twenty-five hundred.

" However, we're over those troubles now. A tank's like a book. First of all you have to get a guy to write it. That takes him quite a while if it's to be a good book. Then the publisher has to read it, and make suggestions, maybe. Then it has to be set up and the galley proof has to be corrected, and then the book proof. And then at last it goes to the printer, and you can turn out copies faster than you can count them. And that's what we are doing here right now, each copy dedicated to Hitler and Hirohito, jointly."

I asked one more question.

" Oh, sure, we have labour troubles all right," he said. " When you employ thousands of hands, selected from fifty-three nationalities—yes, that's the figure—not all speaking English, it isn't easy to make all of them see reason all the time. Not long ago I wanted a hundred men to form the nucleus of a new machine shop. When they arrived they were so old that some of them could hardly stand up. That's because the labour unions insist on a seniority priority. I said : 'We're at war, and you can't win a war with cripples. Send me one hundred skilled mechanics under forty years of age, and send them yesterday!' Well, just twenty-seven of the hundred showed up. They were accompanied by eight hundred peaceful picketers, sent by the labour bosses to make sure I didn't get any more. We fixed things in time, but time's what matters, these days."

All of which seems to add up to this : that when you are engaged in a total war and want to win it, you must deliver the goods, if not yesterday, at least to-day and not to-morrow.

XXVI

AMERICA LIKES TO BE TOLD

Last night I attended a great gathering in New York, assembled to inaugurate the House of Freedom. The House in question is a symbolical edifice, and is merely the new name of the body lately known as the Fight for Freedom Society, which was organised during neutral days in order to wage war against the Nye-Wheeler-Lindbergh Isolationist group, who called themselves the America First Committee. That Committee now lies dead, or dormant, but the Fight for Freedom Society, as its new title indicates, has set up house for the duration.

The meeting was addressed by a notable band of speakers, most of whose names are familiar in British ears. They were Herbert Agar, editor of the *Louisville Courier Journal* and founder of the Society ; Wendell Wilkie, Miss Dorothy

Thompson, Archibald McLeish, and Quentin Reynolds. Mr. McLeish is Director of the Office of Facts and Figures, which, as its title implies, is the nearest American approach to our Ministry of Information. He is young, sincere, eloquent, and should be heard of much in the future. Keep your eye, too, upon Robert Agar; he is genuine Presidential timber, as some of us recognised during a brief visit which he paid to England a year ago.

But the hit of the evening was scored by Quentin Reynolds, the American war correspondent. He will best be remembered in Britain as the commentator in that impressive documentary film, " London Can Take It," and for his even more impressive broadcast addressed to Dr. Goebbels exclusively. He is burly, dark-haired and clean-shaven, and bears a curious resemblance to Wendell Willkie, by whom he sat on this occasion. His speech was a first-class example of sustained invective, and when an American speaker employs invective, he does not mince words. It was addressed to all undercover workers against national and inter-Allied unity at the present time. Here is how he began :

" I have been back home for seven weeks now, after covering various war fronts for more than two years ; and I am a much-muddled man. I was under the impression that we were at war with Germany and Japan. I find here in New York that we are really at war with Britain and the President of the United States ! "

This trenchant thrust, and the roar of approbation with which it was received, reduced to its proper absurdity the recent epidemic of anti-British gossip. I say recent, because the agitation seems to have died down again ; indeed, it was so lacking in foundation, and shot up to such fantastic heights, that it practically collapsed upon itself, and Americans are feeling a little ashamed that it should have happened. Not that it will not happen again, at moments of setback and disappointment. The Fifth Column will attend to that.

This week, too, America has had its first official reminder, from no less an authority than Lord Halifax, in a most timely radio broadcast, of the injustice and ingratitude of belittling British war effort and sacrifice at this time. Our Ambassador spoke for a full half-hour, and was refreshingly informal. He began by suggesting that his hearers should take pencil and paper and make notes of what he was about to say. Certainly some of the facts of which he reminded them must have made many listeners wonder how they could ever have been persuaded that Britain was not pulling her weight, or leaving other people to do her fighting for her. He also referred to our mutual friend Donald Duck, and to the documentary film, recently described in this column, in which Donald is depicted filling in his income-tax form. The special point made by Lord Halifax was that had Donald Duck been a British subject he would have paid, not thirteen dollars on his declared income of twenty-five hundred dollars, but five hundred and fifty.

Lord Halifax dealt faithfully, too, with certain fixations of the American mind—the belief, for instance, sedulously fostered in certain quarters here, that practically the whole of the British Army to-day is living a life of ease in Britain itself. He gave certain figures, explained the difference between regular troops and the Home Guard, and pointed out that when you live upon an island with three thousand miles of coastline, some of it only twenty miles from enemy territory, it seems reasonable to provide that island with an adequate garrison. He might have added that the successful invasion and occupation of Britain at this juncture by enemy troops would practically mean the end of everything, so far as the Allies were concerned, America included.

The Ambassador next referred to our Allies overseas. He made no bombastic claims, but as he traversed the habitable globe from the Arctic to the Equator, making mention of the destruction of two great Italian Armies and of heavy casualties inflicted upon a third " well stiffened with Germans " ; of Ethiopia set free ; of British soldiers holding open the gate to Russia in the Middle East ; of dogged fighting everywhere against heavy odds, and at the end of lines of communication eleven thousand miles long ; the note-takers must have written down a great deal that they had forgotten and a good deal that they had never known—for instance, that " no less than eighty per cent. of our total military production, and every soldier for whom shipping could be found, have been sent overseas."

British air effort was mentioned, too—the fifty million miles covered to date by our Coastal Command, the destruction of over nine thousand enemy planes by the British alone ; two-ton bombs, and increasing devastation among enemy objectives. The activities of the Royal Navy were not stressed in any great detail, for obvious reasons, but some idea of the strain involved upon that Service in the protection and conveyal of essential supplies to British shores alone was revealed in the statement that such supplies totalled forty million tons a year ; and of the efficiency of the Service by the simple statement that less than one in two hundred of the supply ships had failed to reach its destination.

And so on. It was a heartening statement and invaluable at the present moment. " A swell story," was the general verdict. But, but, but—it ought to have been told long ago, and constantly repeated.

I recently quoted Barnum, to the effect that the American public likes to be fooled. But the American public also likes to be told. Naturally, being human, it prefers good news to bad, and various mercenary-minded retailers of information take advantage of the fact. But when you have a tale to tell which combines news that is both good and true, why in the name of common sense do we not tell it? Over and over again during my travels up and down this country, when I have contrived to nail a lie to the counter, or emphasise some unadvertised British achievement, or explain the difficulty, sometimes the impossibility, of taking immediate and final action in this field or that—India, for instance—my hearers exclaim : " But why aren't we *told* these things ? " And I can only answer by inviting them, in their own idiom, to search me.

There are probably two reasons for this restraint and reticence on our part. In the first place we have rooted in our national character a dogged disinclination to ask other nations for recognition or approbation of what we are doing. We are inclined to ask : " What does it matter who gets the credit, so long as we all get on with the job ? " In the second, our authorities are, or were, of the opinion that Americans do not want any British propaganda. If by propaganda is meant blatant advertising of your own country, or, worse still, laborious and obsequious attempts to ingratiate yourself with the people of another, of course America does not want British propaganda. The Americans may like to be fooled, but they are not fools. But circumstances alter cases. Action which would be presumptuous and improper in a nominally neutral country is both appropriate and necessary after that country has become your ally. To-day, for instance, we must counter enemy misstatements, and also reassure Americans that they are being supplied by a willing, efficient, and unexhausted Britain. In other words, America wants not propaganda but information—reliable information—and she wants it all the time. The average

American, what with perpetual radio announcements and newspapers that run to fifty pages on a weekday and a hundred on Sunday, has so much news dinned into him that most of what he hears to-day is bound to be forgotten to-morrow. So, to quote a hymn which I remember singing with great fervour at the age of ten : " Tell me the old, old Story, for I forget so soon ; the early dew of morning has passed away by noon."

It will be asked what provision for imparting British information to the United States is already in existence. I speak, of course, not of information passed direct to the American Government and American press by our responsible authorities in Washington, but of the mental provender available to the average American student of British war effort. The answer must be that the supply is abundant, but its quality is open to question. Something much more dynamic is required.

If it is permissible to make a suggestion founded on considerable experience, two things should be done, and done quickly. The first I have already indicated. We should tell America, and keep on telling America, and do it in the only way which America herself recognises as effective : and that is to go after America with our story and not wait for America to come and inquire for it. Here the American press can be of enormous help. Every American journalist is a born newshawk, and his sole object in life is an " exclusive " story. He has no use for what may be called " omnibus" information ; no more, in fact, than his opposite number in Fleet Street. So cultivate the acquaintance of the American press individually and not collectively ; go out of your way to give each member thereof an occasional titbit for himself ; and the work of enlisting American sympathy towards British effort will be done for you.

The other suggestion is this. Let us employ the visual

approach. During the last war a large number of British service men, both officers and other ranks, most of whom had distinguished themselves in action, were sent to the United States, frankly as exhibits. There was a naval V.C. captain, there were a blinded Highland sergeant, and many others. They were manly, they were modest, and they had obviously seen service. They were an immense success. Without even mounting a platform, except to " dress " it, they achieved more than countless lecturers. There are many of them here in America to-day—sailors whose ships are being repaired, soldiers and airmen, too. They are being made welcome and entertained with traditional American kindness, but no public use is being made of them. Americans love pageantry and martial music ; there is nothing they would enjoy better than to see these men march down Fifth Avenue with a band at their head— a pipe band if possible. Last week, in accordance with inevitable custom, St. Patrick's Day was celebrated here in due and processional form, and all New York donned green favours and went Irish for the occasion. One would like to see them given a chance to go British for an afternoon, say, next St. George's Day.

XXVII

BLACK-OUT IN NEW YORK

THE American people have decided that air-raids upon their country are not by any means an impossibility. This being so, they have to make up their minds what they are going to do about it.

Needless to say there are various schools of thought upon the subject, the thought varying in the main with the geographical whereabouts of the thinker. The great cities of the East and West are as vulnerable as London and Manchester, and are demanding that measures shall be taken accordingly. In the Middle West, a thousand miles from either ocean, public interest in the subject is languid. Between the Mississippi and the Rockies there is no interest at all. In other words, America is a vast country, and her problems of defence bear little relation to those of our own small and congested island. We black out our tiniest hamlet, and with good reason. America feels under no particular obligation to black out the Desert of Arizona or the Grand Canyon.

Two outstanding questions engage the public mind to-day: Which coast is the more likely to be attacked, Atlantic or Pacific? And, How far could such attacks be made effective?

To take the second question first, the general consensus of opinion seems to be that the East Coast is in far greater danger than the West, because the Atlantic passage is much shorter than the Pacific; and because the Eastern seaboard presents far more important and accessible targets than the Western. That, at any rate, is the opinion of the East, and the East is probably right. What the West may think is another matter. In America East is very much East and West is very much West.

As regards the first question, it is calculated that in order to effect a direct transatlantic bombing raid, the enemy will have to travel some three thousand five hundred miles from his French or Norwegian bases, and that to accomplish the round trip and allow the usual margin for bad weather and other emergencies, a bomber must be prepared to fly about nine thousand miles non-stop. Both the Germans and the Italians possess aircraft capable of performing this feat, but two things are obvious: they could not perform it often, and they could not carry a really heavy bomb-load.

There are two other possibilities to consider. One is

that of a "sacrificial" or "suicide" raid, from which the raider would contemplate no return; the other, the establishment of refuelling bases, ashore or afloat, within convenient striking distance of the Atlantic seaboard.

Raids upon the Eastern States, and upon such vital centres as New York, Boston, Philadelphia and Washington, are therefore possible enough, and reasoned opinion here has decided that they are probable as well, if only for their moral effect.

America's problem, or rather the problem of America's exposed cities and industrial areas, is to decide how far the risk justifies elaborate precautions. Obviously it is as impossible as it is unnecessary to set up a system of air-raid defences comparable with those of Britain.

London is liable to be raided heavily and continuously at any time; New York, as the War stands at present, need expect nothing worse than an occasional uncomfortable half-hour. The general conclusion seems to be, and a very sensible conclusion it is, that Americans must be prepared to "take it," adopting only such precautionary and defence measures as may be reasonable. To establish an enormously strong system of anti-aircraft defences throughout the country, keeping valuable artillery and fighter aircraft immobilised perhaps for months on end, or to submit the citizens of the City of Bright Lights to a permanent and depressing black-out, would be to play the enemy's game for him.

Then there is the question of shelters. New York possesses nothing like our providential Tube system, nor does any other American city. All underground railways here run immediately below the level of the street; and I, for one, would dislike intensely to find myself in the New York Subway during an air-raid, especially in the usual close-packed and polyglot Subway company. But New York possesses an unlimited number of concrete and steel skyscrapers, practically fireproof, and it is considered that their occupants, by collecting in the central part of the building, well above the street and well below the roof, will be practically safe from downward impact or upward blast. There are, however, numerous tenements and rookeries in the poorer quarters, as well as innumerable side streets composed of old-fashioned brick or brownstone houses, which would offer no resistance to a direct hit. Provision will have to be made for these.

A regular black-out is not contemplated, but a general dim-out is making itself perceptible. A few traffic-lights now display the small luminous crosses so familiar to ourselves, and in certain streets at night only every alternate lamp is alight. Some of the blazing advertisement signs which render Broadway the centre of New York night life have been turned out for the duration. One enormous sign, depicting a swarm of corybantic goldfish, and consuming enough electricity, it is said, to light a town of ten thousand inhabitants, has been dismantled altogether. My own favourite, the head of a soldier smoking a particular brand of cigarette, with real smoke emerging from his mouth in enormous and regular puffs, still happily survives.

Meanwhile a whirlwind campaign of " defence education " is under way. Trains, omnibuses, and public buildings are placarded with notices telling New Yorkers what to do during an air-raid. They are to keep cool; they are to co-operate with the police and air-wardens; they are not to telephone; they are to get off the streets; they are not to shout. The notices are all signed, F. H. La Guardia, Mayor. So far no actual method of giving an air-raid warning has been devised and sufficiently powerful to overtop the ordinary noises of New York; but experiments with bigger and better sirens are in active and argumentative progress.

In this connection it must again be remembered that democratic enterprise, especially in America, works under two handicaps—the overlapping of authority and the well-meaning assistance of innumerable voluntary organisations. Our dynamic Mayor, for instance, does not always see eye to eye with the Governor of New York State, nor either of them with the military hierarchy. In the field of amateur assistance, countless newly-born societies are competing with one another in the provision of canteens, welfare centres, accommodation for persons rendered homeless by air-raids, and reception centres for lost children. The City Council, too, has just issued a most formidable list of equipment with which the owners or occupants of every building in New York must furnish their premises. In an English town one often sees a friendly notice in somebody's front window : " Stirrup pump kept here." Mayor La Guardia tolerates no such half-measures. Your house must maintain its own stirrup-pump, of a specified make—much to the gratification of the manufacturers of the article in question—together with a large assortment of buckets, shovels, sandbags, patent extinguishers and electric torches, under pain of a fine of 500 dollars and six months' imprisonment. Where everything is coming from is a matter for interested speculation among the Mayor's numerous critics. One of them went so far as to describe the scheme as " a profiteer's heaven." In the matter of its execution the average New Yorker will probably be content, as usual, to regard will and deed as synonymous terms.

Last week the City authorities organised a trial black-out in the lower part of Manhattan Island—everything, that is, south of Fourteenth Street, an area of about five square miles. It includes Wall Street, and the whole of the so-called down-town business district ; the Lower East Side, a thickly populated area which includes Chinatown and the old Bowery; and Greenwich Village, a pseudo-Bohemian colony in the neighbourhood of Washington Square, which sedulously cultivates the atmosphere of the Parisian Latin Quarter.

Co-operation was to be the order of the day, and indeed, if the operation was to be effective, it had to be. The Mayor issued an appeal to all patriotic citizens to do their duty, accompanied by a warning to the Fifth Column to pull their necks in. He himself stood for three hours on the afternoon of black-out day at a street corner, handing out to passers-by copies of a pamphlet entitled " What to Do in an Air Raid."

Night came, and with it zero hour, nine o'clock. Certainly the job was no easy one. More than five thousand street lamps were uncontrolled by a master-switch, and had to be turned out by hand. A considerable responsibility lay upon the detachment of Air Raid Wardens detailed for this purpose, especially since no official warning was to be given, and each warden had to rely upon his own wrist-watch. Altogether nine thousand wardens were employed upon various duties. The police were out to the number of three thousand, thoughtfully augmented by the Sabotage Squad.

The blacking-out of windows was left to the occupants of the buildings, and as no provision had been made for blacking-out material, this had to be effected by the turning-out of all lights. So when nine o'clock struck, everybody became extremely busy. The wardens turned off their street-lamps, the motorists and trolley-car drivers switched out all their headlights and stopped their engines, occasionally at the terse and emphatic suggestion of the police; and the householders, office-workers, shopkeepers and restaurant proprietors plunged their premises into gross darkness, in which they dutifully sat until nine-twenty, when the test ended. To make assurance doubly sure, air-raid wardens invaded the basements of certain buildings and cut off the electricity at the main, thereby depriving the people upstairs of the solace of the radio.

The police authorities mounted to the top of the Empire State Building, the tallest edifice in the world, and supervised operations from an altitude of a thousand feet. The Mayor himself, needless to say, was down below in the forefront of battle, " in a coupé with hooded radio lights and faintly phosphorescent fenders zigzagging through the affected area," to quote the lyric prose of a *New York Times* reporter, " like a stream-lined Haroun al Raschid."

The experiment, though somewhat hampered by " a gaudy half-moon and countless blue and white stars," was voted a success. The Mayor rated the success at a hundred per cent., and added this tremendous and memorable rider : " The Lower East Side of New York to-night spit right in the face of the Fifth Columnists."

Meanwhile, upon the back of my bedroom door in my hotel a printed notice has appeared, telling me what to do in the event of an air-raid. I am to keep calm, take a warm wrap and a pillow, and go and report to Warden Schultz on the ninth floor. Normally, I inhabit the fifth floor.

Well, perhaps familiarity with the real thing breeds a certain fatalism in these matters. I have a feeling that if and when the moment comes, I shall take a chance on the fifth floor—in my own bed.

XXVIII

THE PRODUCTION BOTTLENECK

THE winning side in this War will be the side which produces essential equipment more smoothly and abundantly than its enemy. However extensive the plant, however willing the workers, a single bottleneck can choke the whole flow.

Bottlenecks are of two kinds, material and moral. Sometimes, through shortage, say, of a metal required in the manufacture of a single tiny gadget essential to the radio equipment of a bomber, the bomber, though, otherwise completed, cannot go into service. It has to wait until the missing gadget can be manufactured and fitted; and the same applies to every single bomber upon that particular production line.

Material bottlenecks can be overcome in course of time, and once overcome they do not usually repeat themselves. The material and the job are standardised for the duration. But moral bottlenecks—labour disputes, in other words—are different, and far more dangerous, because no one can foresee their coming or, having disposed of them, guarantee that they will not occur again.

In this connexion Lord Halifax, in a recent broadcast to the American people, was able to point out, with justifiable pride:

"If you add together all the time lost in industrial stoppages since Dunkirk until now, it would represent only one day per man every fifteen years. Or, to put it another way, the number of days lost through Labour disputes in Britain during this war represents about one-fiftieth of one per cent. of the total working time; and that is no more than seven seconds of one working day. I don't think there is much wrong with the spirit of industrial Britain."

And so say all of us. But America, so far, as less cause for congratulation. "In the United States," said a leading New York paper last week, "one concern alone, the United States Steel Corporation, has reported that its loss of production from strikes and work stoppages last year was the equivalent of 300,000 tons of steel, 5,000,000 tons of coal, and nineteen days of ship production. Can anybody blame American public opinion for getting hot under the collar when it contemplates the difference ? "

Why should such things be, to-day of all times ? One reason is that America as a whole has not yet awakened to the stark realities of its present situation ; another is that American Labour is composed of a mixed multitude of nationalities, some of whom do not even speak English ; another is that fifth column and other subversive groups are working overtime. But the real answer to the question is that the United States is half a century behind Britain in the handling of labour problems. In a country nearly forty times the size of our own, this is not altogether surprising.

In our own country Trades Unionism is by this time part of the fabric of our national and industrial life. It is accepted by employers and employed. It is governed by mutually acceptable laws and is exercised, as a rule, in a spirit of fair dealing and common-sense. No group may go on strike or down tools without the sanction of its leaders ; if it does, it is directed to return to work until the grievance can be investigated and, if necessary, adjusted by arbitration. Labour has had a long and hard struggle for its rights, and to-day its hold upon those rights is so secure that it can afford, in times of national stress and peril, to waive them for the time being—work longer hours, submit to extensive dilution, surrender other hard-won bastions—secure in the knowledge that all will be returned without question when the battle is over. In short, British Labour to-day is winning the eternal gratitude of our fighting forces and setting an example to the world.

But in American industrial relations the law of the jungle still survives. The closed shop has never been recognised by the Government or the employers. The labour situation has never been standardised, and though the machinery of conciliation exists, the combatants upon either side frequently elect to settle their differences by more direct methods. Labour goes on strike; Capital hires strike-breakers, and the battle is on.

Perhaps those battles were more frequent and spectacular a generation ago than to-day. I can recollect once being in New York during a strike organised by the drivers and conductors of a street-car Company in Brooklyn, who one day abandoned their jobs without notice and left Brooklyn to walk to work. The Company promptly engaged a force of professional strike-breakers, or " Finks." These gentry are, or were, organised in gangs, perpetually on call, and ready to proceed at any moment to any part of the country where their services might be required. So a bevy of Finks arrived in Brooklyn, and two of them were alloted to each car. One drove it and kept off the strikers, demonstrating with bricks and broken bottles, with his revolver, while the other collected the fares. It must have been an exhilarating journey for the passengers. The fares collected, incidentally, were retained by the Finks as their professional honorarium.

But those robust days are mostly overpast, and the struggle has entered upon a more modern and less spectacular phase, equally disastrous to industrial output and goodwill. Labour Unionism, following the fashion of the time, has become something of a racket. The Union officials are not the conscientious, honourable, and modestly rewarded leaders that we know. They are highly skilled and not too scrupulous politicians, with both eyes on the main chance. They are not there so much to negotiate between capital and Labour, as to employ Labour as an instrument in gouging further profits out of Capital.

Every skilled American workman, if he wants to get a job, has forced upon him the necessity of joining a Union of some kind. That obligation is not unknown in our own country, and there is a good deal to be said in its favour. But to the American workman, membership of his Union often means nothing more than a series of extortions, under the heading of " dues," ranging from the high and frequent subscriptions which he is called upon to pay to the bosses at the top, down to the " entrance fee " which he must hand to someone at the bottom before he can get into the Union at all. The practice extends to all sorts of unlikely corners : a piccolo-player may have to pay somebody a hundred dollars before he can get a job in a particular dance-band. This racket is really not far removed from the system under which a small tradesman used to (and possibly still does) pay a monthly fee to a gangster for " protection "—in other words, as an alternative to having his windows broken or his stock looted by the gangster and his friends. And nobody complains : they accept the situation. It is all part of a system, the recognised system of graft.

Naturally, having to pay so dearly for his membership, the workman demands perpetual " action " from his leaders, and occasionally the leaders have to do something about it. Sometimes they have a justifiable and legitimate claim to make to the employers upon behalf of the men. If they have not, and feel that it is time again to demonstrate their own indispensability and justify their enormous emoluments, they simply make some impossible claim upon the employers, and if this is resisted, call a strike.

Some Labour bosses employ a much simpler and less exhausting method. They make a private approach to the heads of some wealthy industrial corporation, and threaten to call a strike of its employees unless it is made worth their while not to do so ; and the corporation finds it cheaper, as a rule, to pay. The " protection " racket again !

Such are some of the perplexities and frustrations which to-day burden the shoulders of that great-hearted giant, American Labour. For, make no mistake about it,

American Labour to-day is perfectly sound and entirely patriotic. Its devotion to its country, in thousands of cases the country of its adoption, is almost pathetic. But the worker is bamboozled and fleeced at every turn. He has been trained, moreover, to regard all employers of Labour as profiteers and oppressors of the poor, and to regard a strike, usually accompanied by violence, as the natural and only means of obtaining better conditions for himself. This is manifestly a false and artificially engendered point of view, firstly because the American employers of Labour, although there are black sheep among them, as elsewhere, are in the main both just and generous, often philanthropic, in their dealings with their men, and the men themselves are already paid a high—by our standards, a fantastically high—wage. It is no uncommon thing for a skilled workman in America to earn anything from fifteen to twenty-five pounds a week, apart from overtime.

But the American worker, being a patriotic citizen, has no desire to profiteer at a time like this. Being also only human, he does not see why he should work for longer hours and lower wages in order to earn huge dividends for other people. " Put a limit on profits," he says, " and I will work twenty-four hours a day and seven days a week if Uncle Sam asks me to."

And therefore at the present moment the whole question of war output and the abolition of moral bottlenecks hinges upon two considerations—the number of hours to be worked a week, and the allocation of a fair profit to the investor ; and upon these twin problems Mr. Donald Nelson, Director of the War Production Board, is bending his tremendous energy and genius for co-ordination.

Normally an American workman works for forty hours a week. If he exceeds this time, he received extra pay at the rate of time-and-a-half, with double pay on Sundays. Forty hours a week simply means a five-day week. If a man puts in seven days, the enhanced rates for Saturday and Sunday increase his earnings by seventy per cent., considerable pickings for him and a heavy strain on the pay-roll. It is therefore suggested that the working week at normal pay should be fixed at forty-eight hours, with time and a half thereafter. In other words, the man who earns, say, ten dollars a day would now, instead of earning eighty-five dollars a week on a seven-day week, earn only seventy-five, and would have to work a minimum of six days as opposed to five. (An American private soldier works seven days a week and gets forty-two dollars a month.) To offset this sacrifice it is suggested that employers' profits should be limited to six per cent. Probably an agreement upon some such basis will ultimately be reached, and in consideration of the needs of the situation it is to be hoped that there will be no long tarrying.

Meanwhile, as a gesture of goodwill, organised Labour, through its leaders, has pledged itself not to go on strike any more. Unfortunately this applies only to officially declared strikes, and there are more ways of obstructing output than by marching out with banners. As already noted, the makers of a single essential gadget may, and frequently do, suddenly take it into their heads one day that they would like to be paid another ten cents an hour, and march out in a body, immobilising the efforts of several thousand willing workers until the haggle is adjusted. There is also a good deal of what is known as voluntary absenteeism. A big shipping arm has recently announced that about fourteen per cent. of its employees are chronically " absent from work from causes unconnected with illness or family trouble."

But in reviewing these difficulties it is only fair that two facts should be borne in mind. The first is that American Labour is utterly loyal and determined to win the war. The second is that absenteeism and moral bottlenecks are the exception rather than the rule. American industry as a whole is doing a wonderful job, and as soon as certain mutual suspicions have been overcome and certain easy-going slackers awakened to a sense of duty, it will do a more wonderful job still.

Perhaps the most useful stimulus that could be applied to all concerned would be to read them Lord Halifax's statement, already quoted, and remind them that British men and women are working not forty hours a week, but fifty or sixty.

XXIX

THE FIRST PINCH

ONE day last week, about the hour of noon, in Fifth Avenue, during one of its most torrential traffic periods, I beheld the unusual spectacle of an elderly lady riding a bicycle. She did not ride fast, she did not ride well; in fact, she was wobbling about in imminent danger of her life. The unusual, in fact the unique feature of the story is not that she was elderly, not that she was braving the traffic of Fifth Avenue, but that anyone in New York should be riding a bicycle at all. The elderly lady was a portent, a symbol, an indication of the first dawning of war stringency in the United States.

In Britain we are so accustomed to the spectacle of cyclists threading their way unconcernedly through the mazes of city traffic, or impeding the progress, in large and defiant flocks, of protesting motorists along the King's highway on Sunday afternoon, or marketing in a country town with a basket attached to the handlebars, that it is difficult to realise that in America, except perhaps in the case of small children in parks, cycling is an unknown, or at any rate despised, form of locomotion. This land of high wages and cheap petrol is a universal car park. Practically everyone has a car standing outside his home, be that home ever so humble, and at any moment any member of the family may emerge therefrom, to drive fifty miles to the nearest town on a shopping or cinema excursion, or fifty yards to the drug store at the corner of the street, to indulge in an ice-cream soda.

The business man office-bound, the plumber summoned to stop a leak, the young lover of either sex hastening to keep a date, the pastor about to pay a parochial call, the student proceeding to a lecture, the factory worker or bricklayer on his way to his day's work, even the coloured gentleman who has contracted to mow your lawn at fifty cents an hour, each and all drives his own car. (At any rate it will be his as soon as the final instalment is paid off.) In every case, upon arrival, he parks the car outside its temporary destination, to the obstruction of general traffic, until it may be wanted again. That is why it was observed just now that America is one vast car park.

In other words, America never walks when it can drive, which means that America never walks. And therefore to-day America faces her greatest social revolution since the invention of the internal combustion engine. Under the relentless and unpredictable chances of war, a twofold famine has fallen upon this land of easy abundance—a petrol famine and a rubber famine. The latter is the more serious of the two. A synthetic substance is promised, but only in the misty future. Tyres are now rationed and are already practically unobtainable. The best that the authorities can do is to suggest a maximum rate of progress of forty miles per hour, to prevent wasteful wear and tear. And upon the open road in the United States forty miles per hour is a mere cruising speed. So before this war is over millions of cars will be laid up, and millions of Americans, with no experience of self-propulsion since their scooter days, will learn either to walk, sprint for the local train, or ride a bicycle.

The revolution is not yet, of course, fully noticeable, for existing tyres still have plenty of wear in them. The petrol shortage, too, arises to a certain extent from difficulties of distribution rather than actual lack. Still, a so-called curfew has now been imposed under which all petrol stations are supposed to close between the hours of seven p.m. and seven a.m. Voluntary and universal Sunday closing has also been officially recommended. The public response, needless to say, had been mixed, and this has led to a new and original form of guerrilla warfare among competing petrol companies. Recently a chain of petrol stations on Long Island, where New York's Brightons and Southends are mainly situated, dutifully obeyed State instructions and closed down on Sundays, while a rival concern operating in the same territory kept open and did a roaring business in consequence. So the virtuous organisation decided upon a just reprisal. Last Sunday each of the two most important stations of the offending chain found itself besieged by a fleet of cars in need of petrol. So far, so good. Tank-filling in America is a characteristically slick and snappy operation ; the uniformed attendant is screwing on the cap again and handing you your change almost as soon as you have brought the car to a standstill ; so no congestion need be feared. But last Sunday each visiting motorist was in a strangely dilatory and fussy mood. In the first place, no one seemed to require more than one gallon, and between supplying one gallon and ten there is little difference in time consumed, and a ninety per cent. difference in business done. He also asked to have his tyres tested, his oil checked, his water-tank filled and his windscreen wiped. All such little services in America are free. These somewhat lengthy rites accomplished, the motorist produced a twenty-dollar bill and asked for change. (A gallon of petrol costs about eighteen cents.) This manœuvre consumed more time and ultimately emptied the till, necessitating hurried excursions elsewhere in search of dimes and quarters. After that the next car drove up and repeated the performance. By the end of the day the Sabbath-breaking company had sold about one-tenth of its usual supply, received hundreds of dollars and handed most of them back again, leaving the entire neighbourhood possessed of twenty-dollar bills which no one could change. The motto of the company in question is : " Service with a Smile." The stamina of its employees was severely tested upon this occasion.

Of course shortages have not been confined to rubber and petrol. Practically all household commodities are growing scarce, and will grow scarcer, for the industries which produce them are being converted, as with us, to more warlike activities. These shortages, slight though they are at present, bear hardly upon the American disposition. In our own island we are in the main a thrifty and economical race, and when an article shows signs of wear, whether it be a saucepan or a vacuum cleaner, we send it to be repaired. American habit and custom are to buy a new one and hand the old one to the junk-man. There is much to be said for the system on the grounds of trouble-saving and sustained efficiency, but not in times of economic stringency ; and to-day a new order reigns, even newer than Hitler's. The production of such hitherto indispensable adjuncts to the American way of life as radio sets, refrigerators, gramophones, electric razors, even hairpins, is to cease altogether. No more golf clubs are to be manufactured after a given date. This should occasion little hardship, for every golfer in the world has cupboards full of perfectly good implements of the game, discarded from time to time in a fit of exasperation or despair. Old golf balls, too, are being resurrected from dark corners and lovingly cherished. But it may be that as time marches on and the war gets really home, American golfers will be growing potatoes upon their courses, as we are doing.

Clothing is not rationed, but the amount of material per garment is to be restricted. Some rather alarming regulations have been issued regarding male attire. There are to be no more " two-pants suits," which means that the American tailor's benevolent habit of supplying two pairs of trousers to each coat and waistcoat is to be abandoned. That seems reasonable enough ; but the trousers are to be derived of their " cuffs "—what we call turn-ups—and further economies are advocated in the way of jackets without collars or lapels. Samples of these are already on show in shop windows. But a certain proportion of this reforming zeal, we suspect, must be attributed to the advertising enterprise of the individual tailor.

There is much talk of food conservation, but supplies seem to be normal, and the food in restaurants of all grades is both varied and plentiful. Sugar is to be rationed, but as the allowance will probably be not less than a pound per head of population a week, the prospect is not unduly disturbing. Americans still get cream with their coffee— hot milk is never used here—and they drink coffee at least three times a day.

An appeal has been launched for the hoarding of metals and waste paper, and Boy Scouts go round collecting tin cans and old newspapers. Tinfoil is disappearing from cigarette packets, and if you go into a drug store and ask for tooth paste, you must hand over an empty tube before you can be served.

The problem of personnel in hotels, clubs and offices

is more serious, for men are being called up, or going into defence work, every day. An American-born Italian waiter disappears from your ken, and an alien of more dubious neutrality takes his place. A liftboy of my acquaintance, whom I have long and joyfully cultivated as a fountain of unreliable war news and a racy commentator upon life in general, has suddenly vanished, and an elderly gentleman, in perpetual difficulties with the mechanism of the lift, operates in his stead. We spent a protracted *tête-à-tête* the other day, jammed between two floors.

Other restrictions and shortages are making themselves felt. Some are purely sentimental in their effect. There were no Easter lilies, because these come from Japan. There were few hyacinths and tulips in the show windows, because the bulbs come from Holland. Others affect men's very means of existence. " I'm an architect," said an old gentleman to me the other day; " been one for over fifty years. Now all building is out for the duration, except for war work. I guess I'll have to go out of business—unless, maybe, they'll let me design a military hospital. But that's a carpenter's job. I'd best fold."

So there we are. The sum total of it all, as the reader will have realised for himself before this, is that America is beginning, just beginning, to experience conditions which have been familiar to her allies for nearly three years, and is for the moment rather enjoying the thrill of it all. And yet the loss last week of Bataan, with the destruction or capture of its valiant defenders, the most crushing disaster in all American history, has aroused but little public notice or comment. The bereaved are mourning, of course, and the thoughtful are taking more serious thought; but to the many, still undetached from the daily round of business and pleasure, the war and its vicissitudes are still just something to hear about over the radio. It takes time to galvanise a hundred and thirty million people into simultaneous realisation.

XXX

NEWS AND VIEWS IN WAR-TIME

Last week the American Society of Newspaper Editors held its annual conference, or convention, in New York. There is only one real topic of discussion when newspaper men get together in war-time, and that is the Censorship. Once more battle was joined, and some spirited and instructive actions fought.

Freedom of the Press is specifically guaranteed in the American Constitution and Bill of Rights, in which it is laid down that Congress may not " abridge " such freedom. On the other hand, it is generally agreed that in war-time no information must be published which may be of interest to the enemy.

The British and American systems of issuing and censoring news in war-time offers some interesting comparisons. In either case such news falls naturally into two categories —official statements issued to the press by responsible Government officials, and news independently gathered by the press itself. Over the first category no question of censorship can arise, because it has presumably been censored already ; the real tug-of-war comes with the second ; and in connection with America we have always to remember, firstly that the public appetite for " hot news " is insatiable and cannot be resisted, and secondly that in districts of this huge country remote from actuality, where alerts and trial black-outs are unknown, journalistic enterprise is sometimes apt to get the better of discretion ; so the Censor must be eternally vigilant.

The official issue of war news in America suffers, as Mr. Early, the White House Secretary, pointed out the other day, from too much machinery. Nominally the work is in the Hands of the Office of Facts and Figures, but there are other sources of supply not always in agreement with one another. Not long ago, as already mentioned, the Secretary for the Navy and the Secretary for the War Department issued flatly contradictory statements regarding an alleged raid by Japanese planes over the coast of California ; and Congressmen and Senators are also addicted to issuing semi-official and self-inspired items of war news to their constituents. The British method, though cumbrous, does follow a definite plan. Each Government Department, whether military or civil, sends all its news direct to the Ministry of Information. Here it is pooled, collated, and issued simultaneously to the Press and B.B.C. This arrangement is not, or was not, entirely popular with the press, for it gives little or no scope to the individual enterprise of its representatives. However, with the British genius for compromise and making awkward machinery work, a system has grown up by which a newspaper correspondent can supplement his official ration of news by paying a personal call upon the Department concerned, say, the Admiralty or War Office, and picking up a little extra provender, rather richer in journalistic vitamin, from the Department's Public Relations Officers.

But the excess of machinery already noted, and the overlapping of information sources, sometimes makes it difficult for American readers to decide whether a new item is fresh, or mere repetition, or a summary of previous items. In other words, America is getting more war news than it can swallow or assimilate. A periodic and comprehensive review of the war situation, such as our own

Prime Minister is accustomed to give out to the world in his masterly fashion, would standardise public knowledge and steady public opinion. The President, it is true, gives an interview to the press once a week, but as a rule he confines himself to answering questions or planting seeds of future policy.

But to return to our embattled editors. Their general view, not merely of war news but of every occurrence in American daily history, was that " the people of a democracy are entitled to know the facts," and they themselves showed strongly critical of the Government's methods of rationing information. They were not told the whole truth, they complained, and they alleged further that Government officials were in the habit of " adjusting " the news—that is to say, of holding back news of disaster until they could balance it with reports of a more heartening character. " Let the American people have their bad news straight," was their demand. " They can take it."

They also complained of unnecessary censorship, especially of censorship which was fussy and foolish on the face of it—the suppression, in other words, of facts known to millions of people, and therefore inevitably known to the enemy. The burning of the *Normandie* may be quoted here as a case in point. That America's largest and most valuable troopship had been rendered useless by fire was certainly a piece of news of great value to the enemy, and accordingly an order was issued that it was not to be published outside America. But you cannot, it was pointed out, keep secret a prostrate hulk of eighty-four thousand tons lying in New York Harbour for every out-bound vessel to see. Finally this common-sense view won the day, and the news was released, only after a brisk engagement between press and ship.

these indictments the Director of Censorship and

his naval and military colleagues made vigorous reply. First of all they summarised the principles upon which American press news in war-time is officially issued and controlled. Information of naval losses, they explained, cannot be issued until it becomes certain that the enemy is in possession of it, too. A further delay of forty-eight hours is also necessary until next-of-kin have been informed. News of the destruction of enemy vessels, except in the case of submarines, where it is kept secret in order to leave the enemy guessing, is issued the moment accurate information is available. The loss of merchant shipping is announced as soon as next-of-kin have been informed, but no mention is made of the name or location of the vessels involved.

Here, we may note, American practice differs from our own, which is to issue a periodical summary of our shipping destroyed. Possibly that practice has now been discontinued, for no news of British shipping losses has appeared in the American press for some time.

Air losses are fully and promptly reported. Regarding land operations, the usual precautions are observed. Locations and movements of troops are a close secret, and this secret has been particularly well kept. The smoothness and privacy with which enormous bodies of troops have been moved about this country and overseas reflects the utmost credit upon the efficiency of the transport services and the discretion of the American press.

Finally, the extent of losses in personnel are not reported, and no official casualty lists are issued, though casualties may be published unofficially and locally. Here, again, American policy differs from ours.

Answering specific criticisms, the Censor defended stances of so-called foolish and fussy censorship by s that their purpose was to prevent the enemy from em the American press as a " fact-finding mechanis to compel him to rely upon garbled and incomplete rumours. He also emphasised the value of vigilant censorship in preventing the innocent conveyance of information to the enemy. Not long ago a certain newspaper had submitted to it an account of a measles epidemic in a certain camp, quoting actual figures of the number of cases. The story was immediately suppressed, because the percentage of individuals affected in a measles epidemic is a fairly constant quantity; and the figures given would have enabled the enemy to make a direct estimate of the number of men in that particular camp.

The discussion then passed from News to Views, and here the Censorship forces definitely assume the offensive. Editors were warned that in this war voluntary censorship faced its supreme test, and, furthermore, that their enjoyment of it was due largely to the President himself, who had staked his confidence upon their patriotism and discretion. The Censor acknowledged freely that the press as a whole had shown both, but discriminated between the " best of the press " and " the minority." With the latter he dealt faithfully. He said that they were out, firstly, to divide the American people from the British and Russian peoples; secondly, to foment a demand for a purely defensive war and a negotiated peace; and, thirdly, to cause labour trouble and inflame class against class. (He might have added that there are people in America to-day who would almost rather lose the war than see Franklin Roosevelt win it.) He ended by appealing to the honest and loyal majority to cleanse their own household and cast these subversionists from their midst.

So the debate ended—as censorship debates, and, indeed, all controversies in which both sides are very largely in the right, must end—in a draw.

It will have been seen from the foregoing summary that censorship problems in America are not quite upon all-fours with our own. We are a homogeneous nation, and a united nation. Moreover, the voice of experience has laid down just one rule for the relations between the British Government and the British press. Tell the whole story. Reveal the situation entirely ; then specify the particular items thereof which are to be kept secret, and the press will never let you down. But attempt to conceal or garble the facts, and you have challenged every conscientious journalist in your audience to dig out the story for himself. Thus do rumours and misstatements come to birth.

The same rule naturally applies to America, but with a difference. Within that vast and heterogeneous community active enemy agents still function and treasonable newspapers still circulate. Moreover, even among the native-born there are subversive and disloyal cells. This is admitted. So in adopting an attitude of complete frankness towards a press conference, Authority will have to exercise a certain discretion in its choice of confidants. But censorship in America will always be voluntary. The country will see to that.

XXXI

AMERICA GOES TO SCHOOL AGAIN

Most of us remember the study of history and geography as necessary evils of our youth, to be endured at the time and forgotten as soon as maybe. Even in our riper years we are sometimes haunted by vague inaccurate memories of capes and rivers, Kings and campaigns, exports and imports. I still cherish a recollection of a friend of my tenderest youth who, upon being informed by his kindergarten teacher that the principal exports of Norway are pines, beeches, and mahogany, announced to his some-what mystified parents that same evening that the exports in question were " pins, breeches, and macaroni."

But when war comes full circle round the habitable globe, and the nations find themselves bound together in novel and unexpected alliances, history and geography become matters of prime importance. To-day the average American, who has never concerned himself greatly with the history or geography of this world outside his own vast domain, is busy brushing up both subjects. Con-versation round breakfast-tables and in railway-trains is full of unfamiliar phrases, and references to Dakar, Port Darwin, the Irriwaddy, Vichy, the Statute of Westminster, the Indian National Congress. Where are the Solomon Islands ? How far is it from Hawaii to Midway ? How do you pronounce Pétain, Timoshenko, Auchinleck ?

Queries like these are but part and parcel of the perennial American pastime of " Information, Please." Every news-paper maintains such a feature, and practically every radio station holds a periodical symposium on the same lines. (I have to participate in one of the latter, for my sins, next Sunday afternoon.) But during the past few months the American passion for promiscuous and unrelated information has crystallised into something much more specific and much more important. The fortunes and interests of the New World and the Old have become inextricably mingled, and America, with her usual energy, has been busy of late " catching up on " certain neglected studies. The average American, in consequence, has made three discoveries which may alter the whole of his attitude towards world relationships in future, in particular his attitude towards the British peoples.

In other words, he has discovered India, Australia, and France. Or perhaps we might say that he has re-discovered France.

Let us take France first. During the last war, especially during the long period of American neutrality, American sympathies were sharply divided. There was a stout pro-British element, especially in the eastern States and the south, but it was generally considered at the outset that Germany would win, and this naturally strengthened the hands of the pro-German element and strongly influenced the waverers. The Middle West was a German strong-hold, and though the country as a whole favoured an Allied victory, it had little affection to waste upon the British Imperial octopus or the corrupt and despotic regime of the Czar of All the Russias.

But France was another story. France was the traditional friend of the United States. France had sent Lafayette and Rochambeau to aid the young American Colonies in their successful bid for independence, and it was the memory of that fact which kept America, in the main, favourable to the Allied cause during 1914-16. The French, who are quick to exploit an opportunity, especially when it is handed to them on a plate, responded in no uncertain fashion. Perhaps, in their natural desire to conciliate a potential ally, they were inclined to be a little inconsiderate of the feelings of an Ally already in being, and in action, upon their behalf. Members of British War Missions visiting America during those years frequently found themselves sitting upon the platform at some great joint rally for Allied war-relief, listening, with what appearance of benevolent interest they could muster, while some eloquent French comrade-in-arms roused his audience to transports of enthusiasm by recalling the grand old days when French and Americans combined to deliver the American Colonies from the brutal Red-coats.

But that is all over now. France is out. Her rulers have turned back in the day of battle, and made what amounts to common cause with the enemy. Relations, uneasy relations, with the Vichy Government still endure. M. Henry-Haye, the Vichy Ambassador, is still in Washington and de Gaulle remains unrecognised, though he is an ally of Britain. But Vichy is rendering aid and comfort to the enemy to an extent which increases every day. There is the growing menace of Dakar, whence enemy operations may be launched against South American States which America, under the terms of the Monroe Doctrine, is bound to protect from European aggression. Something must be done about Dakar. There is the growing menace of the French West Indies, which if they were to fall into enemy hands would furnish a base for operations against the Panama Canal. Something must be done about the West Indies.

Now, to crown all, Pétain is gone—or going—and Laval has arrived. The situation is critical. At any moment Vichy may take some action which will compel the United States to break off all relations, or even resort to arms. So the average American to-day is keenly studying current French politics, and the geography of what is left of the French Colonial Empire. He has forgotten all about Lafayette, and when an American forgets Lafayette he is inclined to remember that he has other and perhaps sincerer friends, nearer home.

In the second place, America has discovered India. The importance of that discovery can best be measured by contrasting what the average American knew about India three months ago with what he knows now. To him until recently India has been a sort of magnified Ireland—Ireland as traditionally depicted to Americans by Irish politicians in America. His knowledge is derived chiefly from Hindu lecturers, astute and eloquent gentlemen with a heartrending tale to tell of a land of poets, dreamers, and martyrs held down for centuries by a British military garrison and soullessly exploited for British commercial gain.

The Americans, it should be added, are a nation of lecture-goers. With their passion for information and their lack of leisure, they welcome this method of absorbing knowledge in tabloid and predigested form. They are also a warm-hearted and credulous people, with an inherited instinct for personal liberty. This renders them especially susceptible to appeals to their sympathy. A hard-luck story seldom fails to touch their hearts, which is perhaps one of the reasons why they have never expended much sympathy upon the British, who are not good at telling their troubles to other people. But the emissaries of Gandhi and Nehru suffer from no such inhibitions. Their highly coloured tale of woe has scored an immense success, and John Bull has been coming in for some pretty hard knocks of late in the American press and upon American platforms, as British visitors to these shores can testify. "What are you British doing in India, anyway?" "Why do you make India pay a heavy tribute to the British Treasury?" Finally, "Why can't you let the Indians govern themselves?" Even moderate American opinion has urged the British people to seize this opportunity, presented by a common cause and a common peril, to make the supreme gesture of " setting India at liberty."

Then Sir Stafford Cripps flew to Delhi, and America went to school again. Instead of listening to propaganda lectures, the American people began to study the very full reports of Sir Stafford's conferences with the various parties concerned, and discovered, for the first time, that there were two sides to the Indian story.

They discovered in the first place that India is not a single homogeneous country, but a subcontinent shared by several nations, and divided by the sharpest distinctions of creed, language, and political opinion, among whom hard-driven British officials have been striving for generations to maintain a just and even balance. They discovered to their great surprise that India is already largely self-governing, and that each Indian Province possesses a control over its own affairs roughly equivalent to that of an American State. They also discovered, not only that India pays not a penny of tribute to Britain, but is quite at liberty to impose tariffs upon imported British goods.

They further discovered, most surprising fact of all, that the Indian National Congress does not represent India at all (as Congress in Washington represents the United States), but is merely the self-imposed title of a self-appointed political body representing the Hindu section of the population, and taking no account of the great and warlike Moslem population, who despise the Hindus and regard them as idolaters ; or of the numerous Indian States, occupying under their hereditary rulers two-fifths of the soil of Indian, or of the fact that both these bodies would fight rather than submit to the perpetual domination of a Hindu majority.

Perhaps the profoundest impression made at this time upon American public opinion came from a masterly broadcast by Lord Halifax, reviewing the whole history of India, and enumerating the various elements involved in the present problem. The most telling point which our Ambassador made, though he did not stress it, was contained in a brief summary of the Hindu caste system, which lays it down that every individual is born to a fixed status and walk of life in this world, from which he cannot rise or deviate during the period of his existence. Think of the effect of that revelation upon the American people, to whom life, liberty, and the pursuit of happiness are the keystone of their Constitution !

The Cripps Mission may have been a failure in India, but it scored a resounding success in America, because America now knows both sides of the story, and Gandhi, Nehru, and their cohort of lecturers have receded into their proper perspective.

Finally, America has discovered Australia—a continent almost as large as the United States—where Australian soldiers are serving under the supreme command of an American general. The result has been a tremendous " build-up " in the American press of Australian courage and character, all amounting to the general conclusion that Americans and Australians are very much the same sort of people.

A few nights ago, in New York, I attended a great celebration of Anzac Day, the twenty-seventh anniversary of the landing of the Anzac forces upon Gallipoli, at which the new alliance, one might say, was consummated by cabled messages from Mr. Churchill and General MacArthur and speeches from Sir John Dill, Mr. Evatt, the Australian representative in Washington, and Mr. Nash of New Zealand. Each of the latter made a timely suggestion. Mr. Evatt warned his audience against regarding the war purely as an Australo-American campaign against Japan, reminding them of the continued existence of one Adolf Hitler; and Mr. Nash pointed out that as well as the Anzacs, two British Divisions—the Twenty-Ninth and Forty-Second—landed on Gallipoli on the same date.

After that Miss Gracie Fields took charge of the proceedings, and America's education was completed to the satisfaction of all concerned.

XXXII

B . W . R . S .

WHAT do the initials B.W.R.S. stand for? The following paragraph taken last week from a leading American newspaper will furnish a partial answer:

> "Weary, confused, and for the most part in no state to give a detailed account of their adventures, the 290 passengers and crew who formed the entire ship's company, including 37 women and 24 children, of a British liner torpedoed off the coast of Carolina on Saturday, arrived just before midnight last night at Pennsylvania Station, New York. They were greeted by representatives of the British War Relief Society, who promised that by 8.30 this morning every one of them would be fully clothed and provided for."

And it was so.

And here is another story, even more recent. It tells of food and clothing given to the bombed-out people of Bath, described by the American correspondent on the spot as " a perfect old Georgian city." (He might safely have gone several centuries farther back than that.)

> " All basic materials came from the United States. To-day expectant mothers—Bath had a lot of them—received layettes given by women of America. Thousands of warm clothes, shoes, dresses, stockings and underclothes are being unpacked from crates scattered through the stricken city. Hot meals are being cooked on special oil-stoves supplied by the British War Relief Society, which raises all its funds in the United States."

The British War Relief Society was founded during the early weeks of the War—in September, 1939, to be exact—by residents in America of British birth or close British connexion, in order to provide comforts for our fighting forces. But experience soon demonstrated that in total war not every soldier wears uniform; in other words, that a home front can boast as valiant warriors and suffer as heavy casualties as the men in the so-called battle line. A tale of over forty thousand civilians killed in air-raids, and over fifty thousand conveyed to hospital, gave clear indication of many thousands more who had escaped death only to find themselves homeless, destitute, and bereaved. So the Society's activities were promptly extended, and to-day there is hardly a township in Britain which has not received help from the B.W.R.S., and hardly a township in America which has not contributed. Few of the contributors have ever visited our island; they are simply people to whom England, whatever their current opinion of her inhabitants may be, is for ever England. And even though their country is now at war, and their contributions are demanded nearer home, they are still carrying on for us.

Obviously there is no need to describe benefits to people who have received them, but it may be of interest to those recipients to hear something of the vast organisation which has been set up on their behalf, from a looker-on who has been able to study its workings through State after State of this warm-hearted country.

The contributions of the Society to our aid and comfort are both in cash and kind, and to date it has collected and forwarded, in money and supplies, the sum of over sixteen million dollars. Working costs are surprisingly low, a bare eight per cent., for almost every one concerned is a volunteer, serving without pay. The chief expenses are rent, postage, and internal freight charges. Note that word " internal." All carriage overseas is provided free by the British Government, and it is cheering and reassuring to know that no less than ninety-seven per cent. of the supplies have arrived triumphantly at their destination.

The actual funds are raised in an ingenious and systematic fashion. Each city or district of America is assessed by the Society—or assesses itself—as being able to contribute a certain sum, according to population. To the eye of one unfamiliar with the splendour of American generosity, these assessments are astonishingly high. Cities with a population of over a quarter of a million are rated at a minimum contribution per annum of one hundred thousand dollars. Cities with a population of less than a quarter of a million but more than a hundred thousand are assessed at twenty-five thousand dollars, and so down the scale. As soon as a city has contributed its quota, its name is placed upon a Roll of Honour, and published. I recently examined that Roll. Sixty-six American cities and townships had qualified for it. Boston Regional, assessed at a hundred thousand dollars, had contributed something over a million. Chicago, supposed to be the most anti-British city in America, had raised nearly eight hundred thousand. A little town in Florida whose name you never heard of had sent over twelve thousand. Honolulu, in Hawaii, situated more than eight thousand miles from Britain, sent nearly fifty thousand. And be it remembered that these incredible sums are not being raised as part of some gigantic drive for American national war relief or welfare, but merely to help a lot of bombed-out Britishers.

One of the heaviest items of cash expenditure is the maintenance of a complete American Hospital in England, recently renamed the Churchill and transferred from Basingstoke to entirely new premises elsewhere. It is said to be the first hospital ever constructed with a view to withstanding aerial bombing. No need here to carry bedridden patients down to the sub-basement in the event of a raid. The equipment and personnel are entirely American. America has also sent to us more than one thousand so-called mobile kitchens, or Queen's Messengers, available wherever homes have been stricken, and their occupants rendered destitute. A year or more ago, after the great raid upon Clydeside, or rather upon the workers' residential district adjoining the shipyards, a squadron of these kitchens was instantly at hand, and served twelve thousand meals in five days. More of these kitchens are now in North Africa, ministering to British, Anzac, and Free French alike.

The Society maintains great warehouses at all the principal shipping points of America. Here the supplies for overseas are sorted, packed, and labelled, all by volunteers, most of whom are women. Packing a trunk, with its perpetual lifting and bending, is never a light job. Transform the trunk into a deep packing-case and multiply the packing-cases by a hundred, and you will arrive at a good working definition of a labour of love.

But auxiliary aid is frequently and cheerfully forthcoming. The other day, while visiting one of these centres in a great American seaport, I observed a dozen men of our Royal Navy helping with the work. They were lower-deck ratings from a British cruiser lying up in the local Navy Yard for repairs, who were filling in an off-day by contributing their service, in token of their gratitude for benefits conferred upon the brotherhood of the sea in general by the British War Relief Society.

Those benefits are inestimable. In each of twenty-seven ports of the American Eastern Seaboard the Society maintains a British Merchant Navy Club. Here you will always find a gathering of the followers of the most comfortless, the most perilous, and the least advertised of all war-time professions. Many of these are men who have recently suffered what they describe as a bit of a bump —a torpedo, in other words—and have been picked up in some ocean waste, sometimes after days spent in an open boat, and conveyed to one of these American ports to rest and refit, having lost whatever pitiful possessions they ever had. No less than sixty-five thousand garments have been issued to these men.

Others you will meet here who, having recovered from their experiences, or having been fortunate enough so far to escape them altogether, are indulging in the rare luxury of a holiday ashore, where they may indulge in a glass of beer, or attend a cinema, or even dance, all as guests of the Society.

But to return for a moment to our packing-cases. By a happy inspiration, whenever a garment arrives at the Society's headquarters, those bearing a tag, as most of them do, with the name and address of the sender, are despatched overseas with the tag still attached; so that the recipient, if he or she pleases, may write to acknowledge the gift; and in most cases the recipient is more than pleased to do so. Thus a personal contact, a sort of long-distance friendship, is established—say, between Mrs. A. of Plymouth or Whitechapel, and Mrs. B. of Manhattan or Minneapolis; and you can express your thanks and open your heart in these circumstances to an extent impracticable between yourself and the honorary secretary of a corporation, however benevolent.

Sometimes the thanks takes a more tangible form. Not long ago some very small and humble inhabitants of a bombed-out English city received "from America" a parcel containing toys—toys of unimaginable splendour, the gift of happier children more happily placed. They decided that it would only be polite to send something in return. They had not much to send, but what they had

AMERICA COMES ACROSS

they sent. In due course their parcel arrived at the head-quarters of the British War Relief Society in New York, addressed to their youthful benefactors. It was found to contain a soiled and tattered Teddy Bear, a rabbit whose woollen hide bore the marks of affectionate and none too clean fingers, and a much battered rag-doll with a crudely painted cotton face—mute but by no means inglorious survivors of God knows how many air-raids, now offered upon the altar of friendship and gratitude by one set of small persons to another. The ladies who opened that parcel are said to have been moved to tears. They are not alone.

That little story seems to sum up everything that War Relief stands for—human compassion and generosity on the one hand, human gratitude and remembrance on the other. It also teaches us grown-ups a salutary lesson in international relations, at a moment when the one thing we require to render victory certain and inevitable is loyal co-operation and goodwill between Allies—Allies some-times sorely and excusably tempted to criticise one another. So let us see to it that we follow the excellent, if uncon-scious, example of these small diplomats. When we give up arguing as to who is winning the War for whom, the day will be ours.

THE END